Nǐ Hǎo

④

Chinese Language Course

Advanced Level

by

Shumang Fredlein

ChinaSoft

eText – Language Lab software download:
downloads.chinasoft.com.au

Nǐ Hǎo 4 – Chinese Language Course – Advanced Level
First published 2001; reprinted 2004, 2005, 2006
Revised 2008; reprinted 2010
3rd edition 2012

ChinaSoft Pty Ltd   ABN: 61 083 458 459
P.O. Box 845, Toowong, Brisbane, Qld 4066, AUSTRALIA
Telephone   (61-7) 3371-7436
Facsimile   (61-7) 3371-6711
www.chinasoft.com.au

Written by Shumang Fredlein (林淑满)
Illustrated by Xiaolin Xue, Zhengdong Su, Min Huang, Fangsai Mao
Software by Paul Fredlein
Edited by Linda Smith, Sitong Jan (詹丝桐), Christine Ko, Jemma Fredlein

Companion workbook, audio CDs and software are also available.

ISBN 978 1 876739 24 9

Preface

Ni Hao 4 is an advanced Chinese language course for senior school students. A different approach is used for this level. There are more opportunities for listening to unrehearsed text and for discussions in Chinese. Topics for this level reflect the diversity of senior students' lives: from school-based interests and activities to personal/social concerns about health, adolescence, part-time work, relationships, customs, technology and environmental issues.

There are four lessons in this book. Each lesson has three sub-topics and each sub-topic consists of six sections: illustrations, text, data box, short readings, discussion questions and special items. The *illustrations* section has a series of pictures and discussion questions. The pictures reflect the main text and reinforce comprehension. The questions complement the text as a testing tool. The *text* section introduces topics and language to be learnt using dialogue, narration or letters. The *data box*, 资料箱, extends the range of expressions from the text with minimal new words. Partly color coded key sentences are in the cartoons. Students substitute the expressions provided for the colored parts. The *short readings*, 小世界, further reinforce language learnt in the text. The *discussion questions*, 聊天室, are for student conversations. *Special items* include classical literature, short stories, cartoons and puzzles.

Following the three sub-topics are example sentences, vocabulary, character lists and culture information. *Example sentences*, 例句, demonstrate how a particular word/phrase is used grammatically. The *vocabulary list*, 生词, includes new words and expressions from the lesson. New words and expressions other than those from the main text are printed in color and need not be memorized. If they appear in a main text later, they are relisted in black. The *character list*, 学写字, includes characters to be learnt, with stroke order illustrated and radical in color. The *culture information*, 文化厅, introduces culture relevant to the topics.

All characters learnt from Ni Hao 1 to Ni Hao 4 are listed in the last appendix, ordered by stroke number. Students can look up the appendix to recap the Pinyin and to check meanings of a particular character.

*   *   *

I would like to thank teachers Peter Chan, Winnie Edwards-Davis, Beth Hart, Chris Kain, Jessy Tu, Ken Wong and Lin Song, who provided helpful suggestions. My gratitude also goes to Linda, Christine, Sitong, Donald and Xiaolin for their dedication, enthusiasm and hard work. And to Jemma and David for their inspiration, to Paul for his ongoing support, in addition to his software programming. Without them this book would not have been realized.

Shumang, 2007

Contents

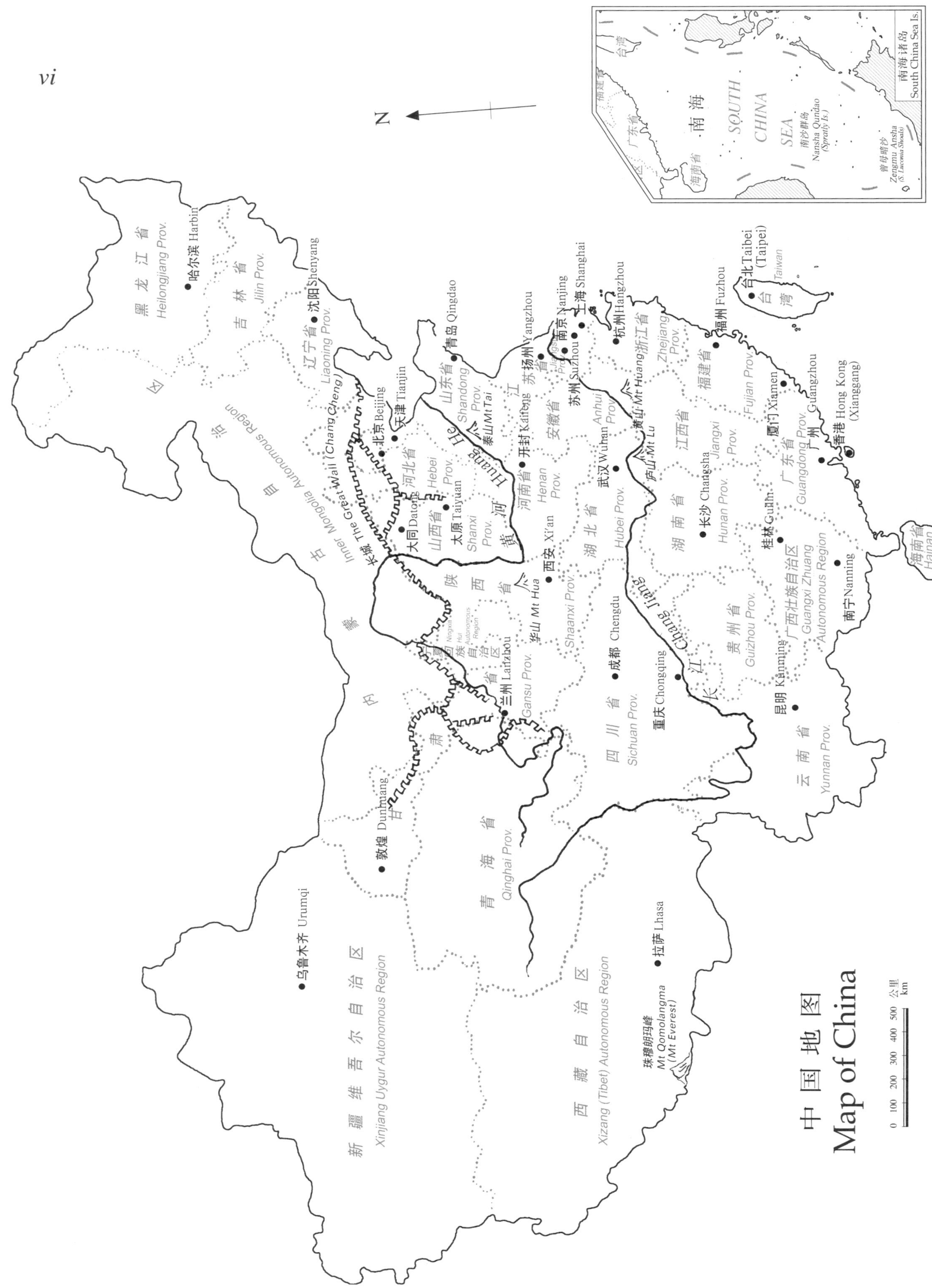

N

SOUTH CHINA SEA

南海

台湾

广东省

海南省

南海诸岛
South China Sea Is.

南沙群岛
Nansha Qundao
(Spratly Is.)

曾母暗沙
Zengmu Ansha
(S. Lacomia Shoalia)

黑龙江省
Heilongjiang Prov.

哈尔滨 Harbin

吉林省
Jilin Prov.

辽宁省
Liaoning Prov.

沈阳 Shenyang

内蒙古自治区
Inner Mongolia Autonomous Region

长城 The Great Wall (Chang Cheng)

北京 Beijing

天津 Tianjin

河北省
Hebei Prov.

大同 Datong

山西省
Shanxi Prov.

太原 Taiyuan

黄河 Huanghe

山东省
Shandong Prov.

青岛 Qingdao

泰山 Mt Tai

开封 Kaifeng

河南省
Henan Prov.

安徽省
Anhui Prov.

扬州 Yangzhou

苏州 Suzhou

南京 Nanjing

上海 Shanghai

杭州 Hangzhou

浙江省
Zhejiang Prov.

黄山 Mt Huang

庐山 Mt Lu

江苏省
Jiangsu Prov.

武汉 Wuhan

湖北省
Hubei Prov.

陕西省
Shaanxi Prov.

西安 Xi'an

华山 Mt Hua

宁夏回族自治区
Ningxia Hui Autonomous Region

兰州 Lanzhou

甘肃省
Gansu Prov.

敦煌 Dunhuang

青海省
Qinghai Prov.

乌鲁木齐 Urumqi

新疆维吾尔自治区
Xinjiang Uygur Autonomous Region

西藏自治区
Xizang (Tibet) Autonomous Region

拉萨 Lhasa

珠穆朗玛峰
Mt Qomolangma
(Mt Everest)

四川省
Sichuan Prov.

成都 Chengdu

重庆 Chongqing

云南省
Yunnan Prov.

昆明 Kunming

贵州省
Guizhou Prov.

广西壮族自治区
Guangxi Zhuang Autonomous Region

南宁 Nanning

桂林 Guilin

长江 Chang Jiang

湖南省
Hunan Prov.

长沙 Changsha

江西省
Jiangxi Prov.

福建省
Fujian Prov.

福州 Fuzhou

厦门 Xiamen

广东省
Guangdong Prov.

广州 Guangzhou

香港 Hong Kong
(Xianggang)

海南省
Hainan Prov.

台北 Taibei
(Taipei)

台湾 Taiwan

中国地图
Map of China

公里
km

0 100 200 300 400 500

第一课　又开学了

1 School's great（开学真好）

Listen and discuss -

1. Sample people's attitude towards coming back to school.
2. Who is the form teacher? Give details of the teacher.
3. Who is the student leader and why was he/she elected?
4. Can the student leader handle the job? Give reasons.
5. What does Li Qiu think of her new friendship?

（一）开学真好

时间过得真快，好像才开始放假，马上又开学了。今天小明在学校非常开心。他说开学真好，放假在家太无聊了。大伟说他有点儿不想回来上课，因为他的心还在北京。

我们今年的班主任是学校新来的汉语老师，他姓张。听说张老师教学认真，也很关心学生。今天他告诉我们："开学了，大家要把心收回来，好好儿学习。"我想，张老师会是一个很好的班主任。

下午开班会时，同学们选了大伟当班长。大家都认为大伟热心，人缘儿好，是班长的最佳人选。大伟说今年学习忙，学校的活动也多，他担心忙不过来。同学们要他放心，告诉他学校的活动大家都会帮忙。

我今天交了一个新朋友，姓章，叫章真。章真是我们班新来的同学。我们俩一见面就很谈得来，马上就成为好朋友了。

资料箱

zī liào xiāng

主任

● 开学了，他的心收回来了吗？

没有，他的心还在北京。

还在北京
还在海边 (hǎi)
还在家里
还在电影院 (yuàn)
还在放假

收回来了。他最喜欢上学了。

最喜欢上学了
学习很认真
是个好学生
觉得放假很没意思
觉得在家太无聊了 (wú liáo)

● 他人怎么样？

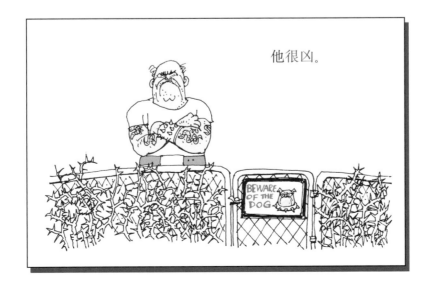

他很凶。

很凶 (xiōng)
很热心
很关心学生
教学很认真
学习很好
人缘儿很好 (yuán)
没人缘儿
很外向
很内向

小世界

收不回来

　　学校开学了，可是黄东南还天天很晚睡（shuì）觉，心收不回来。今年他们的数学老师也是他们的班主任（zhǔ rèn）。他姓高，长得很高很瘦。同学们都说高老师教学认真，也很关心学生，可是黄东南觉得他太凶（xiōng）了。

会帮忙

　　李（Lǐ）平学习好，人缘儿也好。他外向、热心。今年同学们选（xuǎn）了他当班长（zhǎng）。他说："大家有什么事，来找我，我都会帮忙。"黄东南明天要交数学作业，可是他还没开始（shǐ）做，也不会做。他想："李平说有什么事他都会帮忙。我看，我去找他帮我做作业吧！"

忙不过来

我天天都很忙。早上七点半妈妈叫我起床，八点一刻爸爸开车送我上学。在学校，我们有很多功课，也有很多考试。放学后，我先和同学一起打球，再和朋友逛街吃东西。晚上吃过饭后，我先玩电脑，看电视，再给朋友打电话。我十点半开始做作业，把作业做好时都快十二点了。我觉得，我们考试太多，作业也太多了，我忙不过来。

谈不来

王开是学校新来的同学。我们不同班，可是很谈得来，马上就成为好朋友。林明和我是同班同学，可是我们谈不来。我们已经同班五年了，到现在都没成为朋友。

聊天室 liáo

1. 开学了，你的心收回来了吗？

2. 你们的班主任是谁？他／她人怎么样？ zhǔ rèn

3. 你们的班长是谁？他／她人怎么样？ zhǎng

4. 你觉得谁是班长的最佳人选？为什么？ jiā xuǎn

5. 你平常忙得过来吗？都忙些什么？

6. 你和你的朋友谈得来吗？你们都谈些什么？

姓什么

小姐贵姓？

我姓李。 Lǐ

哦！是林小姐。 ǒ Lín

不是林，我不姓林。我姓李，木子李。 mù

哦！是木子李，不是双木林。 shuāng

不是双木林，您听错了。

告诉我，那位小姐姓什么？ gào sù wèi

她姓林，双木林……不，她姓李，木子李。

哈哈……你说，她是姓林还是姓李？ ha

我说，她不是姓林，就是姓李！

Grrrrrrrrr

2 Extremely busy（忙得不得了）

Listen and discuss -

1. When are the school extracurricular activities scheduled? What programs are available?
2. What after-school activities do Li Qiu, Xiaoming and Lanlan have at present?
3. What is the speaker busy with after school lately?
4. What do you think the students feel about their activities?

（二）忙得不得了

　　每个星期五下午是我们学校的课外活动时间。课外活动的项目很多，有足球、垒球、排球、板球和体操等。今年学校增加了划船、空手道和高尔夫球三个项目。同学们都很高兴，大家都可以选到自己喜欢的项目。

　　除了学校的课外活动以外，每天下课后，同学们也忙着自己的活动。李秋今年加入了交响乐团，每个星期有两天要练小提琴。王小明加入了足球队，每个星期得练三次球，又常常要参加比赛。李兰兰下个星期要参加数学比赛，现在天天都在做练习。

　　下个月学校要开游园会。我们班打算摆一个吃的摊位，卖春卷和炒饭。现在我和班上几个同学正在忙着准备，每个人都忙得不得了。不过我觉得，大家虽然都很忙，但是忙得挺开心的。

资 料 箱

● 你参加了什么课外活动？

我加入了空手道社。

我加入了国际象棋社。

Check!

pái duì
排球队

lěi duì
垒球队

bǎn duì
板球队

lán duì
篮球队

pīng pāng
乒乓球队

ěr fū
高尔夫球队

huá chuán
划船队

tǐ cāo
体操队

yóu yǒng
游泳队

xiǎng tuán
交响乐团

hé chàng tuán
合唱团

kōng   shè
空手道社

jí quán shè
太极拳社

jì xiàng qí shè
国际象棋社

● 今年学校有什么活动？

今年四月，学校要开舞会。

wǔ
舞会

晚会

yóu yuán
游园会

运动会

音乐会

小世界

选错项目
xuǎn xiàng mù

　　学校的课外活动，每个学生都要

选一个项目参加。去年我选了篮球，
xuǎn xiàng mù　　　　　lán

还挺有意思的，所以今年我又选了
tǐng

篮球。虽然我喜欢打篮球，但是

我想我今年选错了项目。

参加比赛

　　除了足球队以外，我今年也加
zú duì

入了排球队。今年的比赛，足球
rù pái

在四月，排球在五月。去年的两

个比赛我们学校都输了，今年
shū

我们一定要赢。现在我每个
dìng yíng

星期练三次足球，四次排球，
liàn

忙得不得了。
de dé liǎo

舞wǔ会

今年三月学校开了一个舞wǔ会，大家都玩得很开心。虽然有些同学舞跳tiào得不好，但是也有几个跳得挺tǐng好的。

这个舞会，除了同学们以外，老师们也参加了。我们的数学老师和英语老师舞跳得非常好，大家都看得很过瘾yǐn。

晚会

这个学期汉语老师教我们打太极拳jí quán，同学们都觉得挺tǐng有意思的。汉语老师很高兴xìng，说我们打得很好。七月二十五日学校要开一个中国晚会，老师要我们表演biǎo yǎn太极拳。大家都很开心，现在天天下课后都在练liàn习。

聊天室

1. 你们学校有什么课外活动？
2. 你觉得学校应该增加什么活动？为什么？
   yīng gāi zēng
3. 你参加什么课外活动？为什么选这个项目？
   xuǎn　xiàng mù
4. 你们学校有什么球队？他们怎么练球？
   duì　liàn
5. 学校的游园会你们摆什么摊位？为什么摆这个摊位？
   yóu yuán　bǎi　tān wèi

很 忙

1

○ 今天下课后我们去逛街好吗？
   guàng jiē
● 不行，下课后我有小提琴课。
   tí qín

○ 那么，明天行吗？
● 也不行，明天我有钢琴课。
   gāng qín

2

○后天呢？
●我后天要练空手道。
   liàn kōng

3

○ 这么忙！星期四应该有空了吧？
   yīng gāi
● 我星期四要练网球，……
   liàn wǎng

4

● ……星期五又有小提琴课。
   tí qín

5

6

○我看你一整个星期就只有周末有空了。
   zhěng
●不，我星期六还要练空手道，……
   liàn kōng

7

● ……星期天有游泳比赛。
   yóu yǒng

3 Always on the net（天天上网）

Listen and discuss -

1. How would Lanlan deliver her information to Xiaoming? State the process.
2. What is Xiaoming's recent addiction?
3. What has Lanlan recently achieved?
4. What does Xiaoming usually use his computer for?
5. Why was Xiaoming's father unhappy with him?
6. What does Xiaoming think of mobile phones?

（三）天天上网

小明，我昨天发给你的传真，你收到了吗？

没有，我们的传真机坏了。你改发电子邮件给我吧。

好吧！你的电子邮址没改吧？

没改，不过我有一个新的邮址。我给你新的。

谢了。你那是游戏光盘，是吧？

是啊！挺好玩的。我昨天玩了一个晚上。

你啊，真是个电子游戏迷！我最近设计了一个网页，你看过吗？

没有。给我你的网址，我今天晚上可以上网去看。

你常常上网吗？

我天天上网。除了玩游戏外，我也进聊天室和网友聊天。

我妈妈不准我进聊天室，她说太浪费时间了。

真是的！最近我爸爸也骂我一天到晚坐在电脑前面。

那得看你坐在电脑前面做什么。其实电脑的功能很多，我们应该好好儿利用。

我看手机的功能也很多：除了打电话外，还可以上网、发短信、拍照和听音乐；还有，也可以玩游戏。

资 料 箱

你用电脑做什么？

我上网买东西。

写作业	交网友
学习汉语	上网聊天
设计网页 (shè jì wǎng yè)	上网找资料 (zhǎo zǐ liào)
发电子邮件	上网买东西
玩电子游戏 (yóu xì)	

你常常上网吗？

你常常上网吗？

我不常上网。

常常上网

天天上网

一天上三次网

一个星期上两次网

一有空就上网

不常上网

没上过网

不会上网

你们怎么和朋友联系？ (lián xì)

你们怎么和朋友联系？

我写信、打电话、发传真。

Telepathy.

写信

打电话

发传真 (chuán)

发电子邮件

上网聊天

和朋友见面

 小世界

电脑好用

　　我觉得电脑好用。做作业、上网找资料，或发电子邮件，都很方便。

　　《你好》课本有可以下载的学习软体，练习本也有可以下载的游戏软体。我上网下载了这两个软体，在电脑上自己练习汉语。我觉得游戏软体最有意思了，又可以玩游戏，又可以学习汉语。

电脑不好用

　　现在很多人天天用电脑，上网买东西，进聊天室聊天，或玩电子游戏。可是我觉得电脑不怎么好用。发电子邮件没有打电话方便；上网找不到我要的资料；进聊天室一点意思都没有。听说，电脑还会生病呢！

很浪费 làng fèi

弟弟最近迷上了电子游戏 yóu xì，买了很多游戏光盘 guāng pán。他天天上电脑玩游戏。爸爸、妈妈都很生气。爸爸骂 mà 他天天坐在电脑前面，浪费 làng fèi 时间。妈妈骂他买太多游戏光盘，浪费钱。我说啊 a！弟弟是电子游戏迷。

很担心 dān

黄东南已经一个星期没来学校上课了。我发电子邮件给他，他没回；发传真 chuán 给他，他也没回。学校打电话去他家，他妈妈说因为他爸爸骂 mà 了他，他出去就没回家了。

我们都很担心 dān，就在班里的网页 yè 上放了一封信 fēng，告诉 gào sù 他大家都很关心他，要他马上和家人、朋友联系 lián xì。

聊天室

1. 你用电脑吗？都用来做什么？

2. 你常玩电子游戏吗？你觉得好玩吗？
yóu xì

3. 你常上网吗？通常上网做什么？
tōng

4. 你觉得电子邮件方便吗？为什么？
biàn

5. 你认为电脑最好的功能是什么？
wéi

6. 你们班有网页吗？如果有，都放些什么？
yè

去她家

1

❋ 上次和英英吵架的事，你向她道歉了吗？
chǎo jià qiàn

❋ 我写了一封信给她，可是她没回信。
fēng

2

❋ 打个电话给她吧！

❋ 我打过了，可是她不接。
jiē

3

❋ 发一份传真给她，怎么样？
fèn chuán

❋ 我们的传真机坏了。

4

❋ 我看发一份电子邮件给她好了。

❋ 我没有她的邮址。……
zhǐ

5

❋ 我看，只好去她家向她道歉了。
qiàn

例 句

lì jù

1　School's great　开学真好

才……又……　**just ... again**　It expresses the close occurrence of two events.

你昨天才迟到，今天又迟到了。

姐姐上午才买一双新鞋，下午又买了一双。

也　**also**

我们考试太多，作业也太多了。

她是个网球迷，也是个足球迷。

把　把 literally means "hold", but acts as an indicative word here. It introduces an object ahead of a verb to indicate how the object is dealt with, i.e.,

S + V + O　　　　　　　　　S + 把 O + V

他做好作业了。　　　　　　他把作业做好了。

大家拿课本出来。　　　　　大家把课本拿出来。

翻书到第五十九页。　　　　把书翻到第五十九页。

给我那枝笔。　　　　　　　把那枝笔给我。

选　**to elect, to choose**

今天同学们选了我当班长。

你今年选了什么课？

我今年选了科学和地理。

当　**to work as, to serve as, to be**

她姐姐想当医生。

弟弟今年当了班长。

20

例句

1

过来　(1)　**to come over**

请你过来一下。

他为什么不过来？

(2)　忙得过来　"过来" indicates that it is possible to manage. 忙不过来 is used when it is impossible to manage.

工作这么多，你忙^{de}得过来吗？

还好，我还忙得过来。

工作太多了，我忙不过来。

一 … … 就　**no sooner … than; as soon as**

弟弟病了，一吃东西就吐^{tù}。

哥哥一回家就开冰箱^{bīng xiāng}。

你一来他就走了。

除了……以外　(1)　**in addition to, besides**　It is often followed by "还" or "也".

他除了打篮^{lán}球以外，还打板^{bǎn}球。

我们班主^{zhǔ}任^{rèn}除了教汉语以外，也教数学。

除了我以外，我弟弟也要去。

(2)　**except**　It is often followed by "都".

除了小明以外，大家都来了。

除了你以外，大家都要去看电影。

除了下雨天以外，我天天都去游泳^{yóu yǒng}。

着　v/adj + **着**　"着" is used here to indicate a continuing state, or an action in progress.

考试快到了，大家都在忙着学习。

爸爸天天忙着上班、工作。

快点儿！大家都等着你呢！

得　得 can be pronounced in various ways which represent different meanings:

　　[děi] – **must, need**

考试快到了，我得好好儿学习。

今天家里有事，我得早点儿回家。

明天我不能出去玩儿，因为我得准备考试。

　　[dé] – **to get, to obtain**

昨天的数学考试，我得了一百分。

这次的足球赛，我们学校得了第一。

　　[de] – v + **得**　used after a verb or an adjective to indicate a degree or a result

他走路走得很快。

我妈妈菜做得很好。

我最近忙得不得了。

正在　**in process of**　It may be replaced by "在" but "正在" carries a stronger emphasis.

妈妈正在厨房里忙着做饭。

她正在做功课，不要去打扰她。

他正在睡觉，你找他有什么事？

我们正在吃饭，来一起吃吧！

22

例句

1

不得了　**extremely, exceedingly**　Often follows a 得 to form "……得不得了".

　　我今天没吃早饭，现在饿得不得了。
　　　　　　　　　　　　dé liǎo

　　他爸爸凶得不得了。
　　　　xiōng

　　我们最近忙得不得了。

虽然……但是……　**although ... yet**

　　他虽然加入了足球队，但是不常去练球。
　　　　　rù zú duì　　　　　　　liàn

　　虽然学校有很多活动，但是他什么都没参加。

　　虽然上午天气很好，但是下午下了大雨。

3　Always on the net　天 天 上 网

发　**to send out (fax/e-mail)**

　　我昨天发了一份传真给北京的朋友。
　　　　　　fèn chuán

　　写信太慢了，你发传真给他吧！
　　　　màn　　　　chuán

　　我常发电子邮件给朋友。

一天到晚　**from morning till night, all day long**

　　姐姐一天到晚打电话聊天。

　　弟弟一天到晚玩电子游戏。
　　　　　　　　　yóu xì

　　爸爸一天到晚骂我们。
　　　　　　　　mà

其实　[qíshí] **actually**

　　他看起来有点凶，其实人很好。
　　　　　　xiōng　qí shí

　　弟弟说他作业做好了，其实他还没做。

　　妈妈说我上网聊天，其实我是在做作业。

生 词 ^{cí}

1 School's great　开学真好

开学	kāixué	v. school starts　开 - to open, to operate
才	cái	adv. just, only just
开始	kāishǐ	v. begin, start　开 - to open, to operate; 始 - to start
放假	fàngjià	v. have a holiday or vacation, e.g. 放暑假 - have summer vacation　放 - to put, to let go
开心	kāixīn	v. feel happy, rejoice　开 - to open; 心 - heart
有点儿	yǒudiǎnr	adv. a bit, somewhat
心	xīn	n. heart, mind
班主任	bānzhǔrèn	n. form teacher, homeroom teacher　said 导师 dǎoshī in Taiwan　班 - class; 主任 - director, head; 导 - to guide
听说	tīngshuō	v. be told, hear of, it is said　听 - to listen; 说 - to speak
关心	guānxīn	v. care about　关 - to close; 心 - heart
告诉	gàosù	v. tell, let know　告 - inform; 诉 - tell, appeal to
把	bǎ	prep. indicative word, see p. 19
收	shōu	v. to collect, to receive
班会	bānhuì	n. class meeting　会 - n. meeting; v. able to, likely to
选	xuǎn	v. choose, elect
当	dāng	v. be, work as, serve as, e.g. 当班长 - be a class leader, 当老师 - be a teacher
班长	bānzhǎng	n. class leader　长 - [zhǎng] leader, chief; [cháng] long
认为	rènwéi	v. think, consider　认 - to recognize; 为 - to be
热心	rèxīn	adj. enthusiastic　热 - hot; 心 - heart
人缘儿	rényuánr	n. relations with people; popularity　缘 - predestined relationship
佳	jiā	adj. good, fine
人选	rénxuǎn	n. candidate　选 - to choose, choice
活动	huódòng	n. activity　活 - to live, alive; 动 - to move
过来	guòlái	(1) v. come over, e.g. 你过来。 (2) used after a verb, preceded by "得" to indicate possibility, see p. 20
放心	fàngxīn	v. stop worrying, be at ease　放 - to let go, to put; 心 - heart
帮忙	bāngmáng	adj. helpful; v. help　帮 - to help, to assist; 忙 - busy
交	jiāo	v. to cross, to interact; to hand in, e.g. 交朋友 - to make friends, 交作业 - to hand in homework
章	Zhāng	n. a surname; [zhāng] chapter
见面	jiànmiàn	v. to meet, see　见 - to see; 面 - face, [word ending]
谈得来	tán de lái	v. get along well, usually have a good time chatting　谈 - to talk, to chat
成为	chéngwéi	v. become　成 - to become; 为 - to be
资料	zīliào	n. data, information　资 - capital, fund; 料 - material

生词

箱	xiāng	*n.* box
海边	hǎibiān	*n.* seashore, seaside, beach　海 - sea; 边 - side
电影院	diànyǐngyuàn	*n.* cinema　电影 - movie; 院 - courtyard; compound
世界	shìjiè	*n.* world　世 - world; 界 - boundary
逛街	guàngjiē	*v.* go window-shopping, stroll around the street
聊天室	liáotiān shì	*n.* chat room
例句	lìjù	*n.* example sentence　例 - example; 句 - sentence
鞋	xié	*n.* shoes
翻	fān	*v.* turn over
页	yè	*n.* page
枝	zhī	*m.w.* [for pens, pencils, etc.]
吐	tù	*v.* to vomit, throw up
生词	shēngcí	*n.* new word　生 - unfamiliar, raw; 词 - word, term

2　Extremely busy　忙 得 不 得 了

不得了	bùdéliǎo	*adv.* extremely, exceedingly, see p. 22　了 liǎo - end, result
课外	kèwài	*adj.* extracurricular
项目	xiàngmù	*n.* item
垒球	lěiqiú	*n.* softball　垒 - base, rampart
排球	páiqiú	*n.* volleyball
体操	tǐcāo	*n.* gymnastics　体 - body; 操 - exercise
等	děng	*pron.* and so on, and so forth; *v.* wait
增加	zēngjiā	*v.* add, increase　增 - to increase; 加 - to add
划船	huáchuán	*n.* rowing; *v.* row a boat　划 - to row; 船 - boat
空手道	kōngshǒudào	*n.* karate　空 kōng - empty, kòng - free time; 手 - hand; 道 - method, way
高尔夫球	gāo'ěrfūqiú	*n.* golf [transliteration]
高兴	gāoxìng	*adj.* happy　高 - high, tall; 兴 - cheerful
除了……以外	chúle...yǐwài	*prep.* 1. besides, in addition to; 2. except
着	zhe	*part.* used to indicate a continuing state, or an action in progress
加入	jiārù	*v.* join in　加 - to add; 入 - to enter
交响乐	jiāoxiǎngyuè	*n.* symphony
团	tuán	*n.* group, organization
练	liàn	*v.* practise, e.g. 练球 - to practise ball game; 练小提琴 - to practise violin
队	duì	*n.* team, group
练习	liànxí	*n.* exercise; *v.* practise　练 - to practise; 习 - to practise
游园会	yóuyuánhuì	*n.* fete　游 - to wander, to swim; 园 - garden; 会 - *n.* gathering, meeting; *v.* be able to
摆	bǎi	*v.* set up, arrange, place
摊位	tānwèi	*n.* stand, stall　摊 - stall, stand; 位 - location
班上	bānshàng	in the class
正在	zhèngzài	*adv.* in process of (indicates an action is in progress), see p. 21
虽然	suīrán	*conj.* although
但是	dànshì	*conj.* but, yet, still, nevertheless

合唱团	héchàngtuán	*n.* choir　合 - to combine; 唱 - to sing; 团 - group
社	shè	*n.* club or society of special interest or purpose
国际象棋	guójì xiàngqí	*n.* chess　国际 - international; 象棋 - Chinese chess
舞会	wǔhuì	*n.* dance party
运动会	yùndònghuì	*n.* sports carnival　运动 - sports
输	shū	*v.* lose; be beaten
赢	yíng	*v.* win; beat
过瘾	guòyǐn	*adj.* enjoy oneself to the full
表演	biǎoyǎn	*v.* to perform an act
快点儿	kuàidiǎnr	*v.* hurry up
打扰	dǎrǎo	*v.* disturb

3　Always on the net　天 天 上 网

上网	shàng wǎng	*v.* get on the internet　上 - *v.* to go to; 网 - net
传真	chuánzhēn	*n.* facsimile　传 - to transmit; 真 - real
改	gǎi	*v.* change
电子	diànzǐ	*n.* electronic, e-
邮件	yóujiàn	*n.* mail, e.g. 电子邮件 - e-mail　邮 - mail; 件 - document, a measure word
邮址	yóuzhǐ	*n.* mail address, e.g. 电子邮址 - e-mail address　邮 - mail; 址 - address
游戏	yóuxì	*n.* game, e.g. 电子游戏 - computer game, video game
光盘	guāngpán	*n.* CD, DVD or VCD, called 光碟 guāngdié in Taiwan
设计	shèjì	*v. & n.* design　设 - to establish; 计 - to calculate
网页	wǎngyè	*n.* web page　网 - net; 页 - page
网址	wǎngzhǐ	*n.* website　网 - net; 址 - address
聊天	liáotiān	*v.* chat, e.g. 聊天室 - chat room　聊 - to chat; 天 - sky, day
网友	wǎngyǒu	*n.* internet friend
不准	bùzhǔn	*v.* not allow, forbid
浪费	làngfèi	*v.* waste; *adj.* wasteful　浪 - wave; 费 - to spend, wasteful
骂	mà	*v.* scold, condemn
其实	qíshí	*adv.* actually, in fact　其 - that, such; 实 - fact, real
功能	gōngnéng	*n.* function　功 - merit; 能 - ability, be able to
利用	lìyòng	*v.* use, make use of　利 - sharp, to benefit; 用 - to use
拍照	pāizhào	*v.* take a picture　拍 - to pat; 照 - photo
联系	liánxì	*v.* contact, get in touch with　联 - to relate; 系 - to relate to
好用	hǎoyòng	*adj.* be convenient to use
资料	zīliào	*n.* data, information　资 - capital, fund; 料 - material
方便	fāngbiàn	*adj.* convenient　方 - direction, area; 便 - [biàn] convenient, urine or excrement, [pián] cheap
软体	ruǎntǐ	*n.* software　软 - soft; 体 - body
下载	xiàzǎi	*v.* download　载 - to load
封	fēng	*m.w.* [for letter] e.g. 一封信 - a letter
慢	màn	*adv. & adj.* slow
着急	zháojí	*v.* feel worried

学写字

Radical in color

才 cái *just, only just*	放 fàng *to put, to let go*	非 fēi *not, un-*	心 xīn *heart*	新 xīn *new*
姓 xìng *family name*	听 tīng *to listen, to hear*	教 jiāo; jiào *to teach*	认 rèn *to recognize*	关 guān *to close*
把 bǎ *[indicative word]*	当 dāng *to be, to serve as*	忙 máng *busy*	活 huó *to live; alive*	帮 bāng *to help, to assist*
谈 tán *to talk, to chat*	成 chéng *to become*	每 měi *every, each*	己 jǐ *oneself*	除 chú *except, besides*
着 zhe *[grammatical word]*	正 zhèng *straight, exact*	虽 suī *although*	然 rán *like that*	但 dàn *but*
网 wǎng *net*	邮 yóu *mail*	聊 liáo *to chat*	室 shì *room*	脑 nǎo *brain*
功 gōng *merit; effort*	应 yīng *should*	该 gāi *should*	利 lì *sharp; smoothly; to benefit*	用 yòng *to use*

文化厅

❀ Chinese surnames

Chinese surnames have been passed down through generations over thousands of years. The book 百家姓 Bǎijiāxìng *One Hundred Surnames* listed 504 surnames, mostly single characters with 60 being compound characters. While some surnames are rare, many have been commonly shared. 李 Lǐ, 王 Wáng and 张 Zhāng are among the most popular surnames.

The Chinese commonly address people by their surnames, i.e. 李先生, 王太太, or 张小姐. To ask for a surname, say 你姓什么？ and to answer, say 我姓 .... A more formal way is to ask 您贵姓 nín guì xìng? and to answer 敝姓 ...... bì xìng xx, literally 'your precious surname' and 'my humble surname'.

Some surnames share the same pronunciation but are in different characters, such as Zhāng in 张 and 章. Some surnames may cause confusion when spoken softly, such as 李 Lǐ and 林 Lín. To identify a surname, use 哪个, i.e. 哪个黄？ To respond, one can refer it to a character in a word, i.e. 黄色的黄, or explain the character structure, i.e. 草头黄 cǎotóu huáng, the Huang with a grass radical. The following are examples of common expressions.

Stating the character in a word:

高，高兴的高
王，国王的王
黄，黄色的黄
白，白色的白

Stating the structure of the character:

张，弓长张　gōng cháng zhāng
章，立早章　lì zǎo zhāng
林，双木林　shuāng mù lín
李，木子李　mù zi lǐ
吴，口天吴　kǒu tiān wú

❀ Chinese chess

Chinese chess 象棋 xiàngqí is a popular leisure pastime. Two Chinese men playing 象棋 in a park or a public ground is a common scene. The term 象棋 appears in documents as early as 战国时期 Zhànguó Shíqí the Warring States Period (403 ~ 221 BC). Some suggest that a form of Chinese chess spread to India at around the 8th century which later evolved into Western chess. By the 13th century, 象棋 had been played similar to it is today.

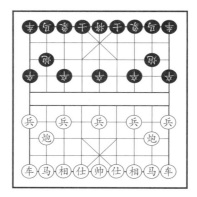

To play 象棋, place the pieces on the line intersections. Its aim is to catch the general. Rules are shown below:

将 jiàng, 帅 shuài (general) move one step, vertically or horizontally, within your castle	
士 shì, 仕 shì (officer) move one step, diagonally, within your castle	
象 xiàng, 相 xiàng (minister) move two steps, diagonally, within your territory, provided there is not a piece in midway	
车 jū, 俥 jū (carriage) move any number of steps, vertically or horizontally, provided there are no pieces in the way	
马 mǎ, 馬 mǎ (horse) move diagonally to the immediate adjoining square, provided there is not a piece on its side along the joining line	
包 pào, 炮 pào (cannon) move any number of steps, vertically or horizontally, provided there are no pieces in the way; when catching an enemy you must jump over one piece	
卒 zú, 兵 bīng (soldier) move one or two steps initially, then move one step forward only within your territory, vertically or horizontally in your enemy's territory	

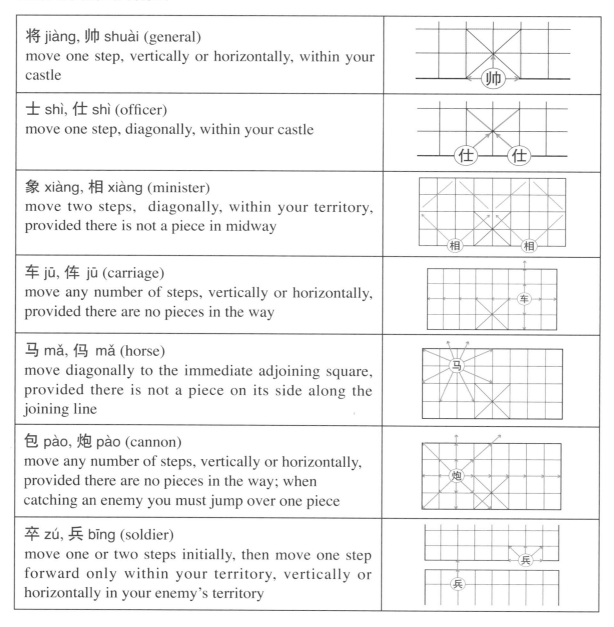

When watching a chess game, people often have an urge to offer advice. The Chinese have a saying for chess observers, 观棋不语真君子 Guān qí bù yǔ zhēn jūnzǐ, *a real gentleman remains silent while watching a chess game.*

✿ Printing and typing in Chinese

The earliest Chinese writing found was inscribed on oracle bones and turtle shells, called 甲骨文 jiǎgǔwén. Much earlier work was written on bamboo slips or silk cloth, using 毛笔. Paper was invented by 蔡伦 Cài Lún (61 ~121 AD) in 东汉, the East Han Dynasty. A Buddhist script printed on paper in 868 AD in 唐朝, the Tang Dynasty, is the earliest reproduction print work that survives. The script was carved on large wooden blocks and then stamped, the same way the Chinese people use personal stamps.

A paper making process illustrated in " 天工开物 ", a science book written in the seventeenth century.

A typesetting method was invented by 毕升 Bì Shēng in the 11th century in 宋朝, the Song Dynasty. 毕升 carved Chinese characters on individual clay blocks and set them together for printing. This method is similar to that of Gutenberg's in Germany that dated around 400 years later. However, typing in Chinese has long belonged to the professionals, even after the typewriter was invented. Locating one character from thousands was an intricate job.

The arrival of the computer revolutionized Chinese typing. It became possible for ordinary people to use, although its input systems vary immensely. To type a character, one can key in its sound, its radical, its stroke order or even the shape of its four corners. Listed below are a few commonly used methods:

拼音 pīnyīn – Type in Pinyin and then select the desired character from the pop-up list of characters. Improvements can be made by

using a word bank. This method is commonly used by people in China as well as Chinese language learners.

五笔 wǔbǐ – Type in the stroke order and then select the desired character from the list. The strokes of all characters are in five categories and represented by numbers one to five. It is a method commonly used by people in China, favored by those not familiar with Pinyin.

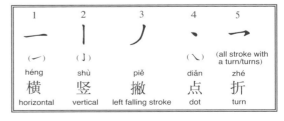

注音符号 zhùyīn fúhào – Type in a phonetic symbol and then select the desired character from the list. Certain keys on the keyboard are assigned to certain symbols. This method is commonly used in Taiwan.

部首 bùshǒu – Type in the radical and other component/s. Certain keys on the keyboard are assigned to certain radicals. This method is also commonly used in Taiwan.

Though not as common as the ones listed above, there are many other methods in use, especially with the mobile phone text message input system. Different companies use different input systems, and all of them claim to have the best system.

1

该来的不来

老王很不会说话。

他生日那天，他请了很多人去他家吃饭。吃饭的时间到了，可是有一些客人还没来。老王很着急，说："为什么该来的人还不来？" 这些来了的客人听了，心想："那么我们是不该来的人啦！" 所以有很多人走了。老王看到那么多人走了，更着急了，说："为什么不该走的人走了？" 这些没走的客人听了，心想："那么我们是该走的人啦！" 所以他们也都走了，只有老王最好的朋友小李没走。小李知道老王很不会说话，他告诉老王："你说错话了，大家都认为你不欢迎他们。" 老王说："我说错话了？我不欢迎的不是他们！" 小李听了很生气，说："那么你不欢迎的是我啦！" 最后小李也走了。

第二课　有朋自远方来

1 When in Rome do as the Romans do（入乡随俗）

rù xiāng suí sú

Listen and discuss -

1. Who is the visitor and what is he like?
2. What impression does he have of this place?
3. What is Dawei's impression of China?
4. What is the visitor determined to do during this trip?

（一）入乡随俗

　　这个学期，学校有一位北京来的交换老师，黄老师。大伟今天下课后去和黄老师打招呼。黄老师很外向，和大伟无所不谈。他们谈天气，谈旅行，谈对各地的印象。

　　黄老师告诉大伟他对这儿的印象很好。他说这儿的人友善，空气新鲜，气候宜人；还有交通也很好，车会让行人。大伟告诉黄老师他对中国的印象很深。他说桂林的风景十分优美，空气也新鲜；北京虽然空气比较差，车也不让行人，但是名胜古迹多，小吃也多。

　　大伟说他喜欢到世界各地旅行，体验不同的风土人情，吃各种不同的菜。黄老师说他也喜欢旅行，不过他不习惯吃西方菜。他以前和旅行团去西方国家旅行时，多半到中国饭馆吃饭。这次他自己一个人来，一定要入乡随俗，学习吃西方菜。

资 料 箱

你对那儿印象怎么样？

印象很深 (shēn)

印象很好

印象不错

印象还可以

印象不太好

印象很差

没什么印象

一点儿印象都没有

你觉得这儿的交通怎么样？

交通很好

交通很差

车会让行人 (ràng)

车不让行人

车开得很快

车常闯红灯 (chuǎng dēng)

常常堵车 (dǔ)

自行车很多

这里的风土人情怎么样？ (tǔ qíng)

空气很好 (kōng)

气候宜人

风景优美 (jǐng yōu měi)

古迹很多 (gǔ jì)

小吃很多

人很友善 (shàn)

人不友善 (shàn)

人很好客 (hào)

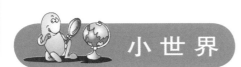

小世界

印象不错

问：听说你们家住了一个交^{huàn}换学生，是吗？

答：是啊！是上海来的交换学生。我妈妈说
我们可以利用这个机会练习普^{pǔ}通话。

问：他人怎么样？

答：他人挺^{tǐng}好的，不过话很少，也吃得
不多。他虽然乒乓^{pīng pāng}球打得不错，但是
小提琴拉^{tí qín lā}得很差。

问：他对这儿的印象怎么样？

答：不错。他不常出^{chū}去玩儿，可是他常说
这儿空气新鲜^{kōng xiān}，人友善^{shàn}，车也会让^{ràng}
行人。

很随便^{suí biàn}

我这个人很随便^{suí biàn}。我什么菜都
吃，住的也不挑剔^{tiāo ti}。我到哪里都能
入乡随俗^{rù xiāng suí sú}。

印象不太好

问：　你是上海来的交换学生，是吗？

答：　是啊，学校放暑假，我利用机会来这儿
　　　学习英语。我现在住在一个同学家。

问：　他们一家人怎么样？

答：　他们都对我很好，喜欢和我聊天，打
　　　乒乓球。不过我担心我练习英语的机会
　　　不多。

问：　你对这儿的印象怎么样？

答：　不太好。这儿的公共汽车少，要出去玩
　　　很不方便。我不习惯吃西方菜，很想家，
　　　想家的时候就拉小提琴。

不习惯

　　我喜欢吃家里的菜，睡自己
的床。出去旅行时，我很不习惯，
常常吃不饱也睡不好。

聊天室

1. 你们学校有交换^{huàn}学生／老师吗？是从^{cóng}什么地方来的？

2. 什么地方给你的印象最深^{shēn}？为什么？

3. 你觉得这儿的交通怎么样？

4. 你觉得这儿的空^{kōng}气怎么样？风景^{jǐng}怎么样？

5. 你喜欢旅行吗？为什么？

6. 你常不常吃中国菜？吃得习惯吗？

路过

……

● 请进^{jìn}，请进，不知道你要来。

○ 路过，进来看看你。

● 喝咖^{kā}啡^{fēi}吗？

○ 不！不！

● 那么，喝茶吗？

○ 不喝！不喝！

● 喝果汁^{zhī}吧？

○ 不用！不用！

○……再见！

……

2 Barbecue in the park（到公园烤肉）

Listen and discuss -

1. Where does the exchange teacher stay and why does the family host him?
2. What was the event and who attended?
3. When and where did the event take place?
4. List the food and drinks provided.
5. How did everyone enjoy the day?
6. What thoughts did the teacher have from this event? Give details.

（二）到公园烤肉

　　黄老师这个学期住在小明家。小明的父母亲希望小明能利用这个机会多练习普通话。

　　上个星期六，他们一家人请了黄老师和几个朋友到附近的公园烤肉。他们准备了很多东西：吃的有香肠、牛排、肉串、面包、沙拉和水果；喝的有咖啡、可乐和啤酒。这天不冷也不太热，是烤肉的好天气。大家一边吃一边聊天儿，有的坐着，有的站着，感觉很自在，不拘束。黄老师觉得请客人到公园烤肉实在很方便。

　　客人走了以后，他们开始收拾东西。小明把垃圾丢到垃圾桶里，黄老师也要把空瓶子和空罐子丢到垃圾桶里。小明的妈妈说：“不，黄老师，瓶子、罐子和塑料袋都可以回收再利用，把它们放到回收桶里。”黄老师心里想：“这家人十分重视环保，回收做得很好。”

　　东西收拾好了以后，大家就一边聊天儿，一边走路回家。

资 料 箱

● 你怎么请朋友吃饭？

我请他们到家里吃火锅。

到家里吃火<ruby>锅<rt>guō</rt></ruby>

到家里吃饭

到家里<ruby>包<rt>bāo</rt></ruby>饺子

到公园烤肉

到饭馆吃饭

到<ruby>饮<rt>yǐn</rt></ruby>茶<ruby>楼<rt>lóu</rt></ruby>饮茶

到小吃<ruby>店<rt>diàn</rt></ruby>吃小吃

● 家里烤肉时，他做什么？

他帮忙烤肉。

帮忙烤肉

帮忙收拾东西

去打球

就是吃

就是聊天儿

就是玩电子<ruby>游<rt>yóu</rt></ruby><ruby>戏<rt>xì</rt></ruby>

就是玩手机

● 什么东西可以回收？

空瓶子可以回收。

<ruby>空瓶子<rt>kōng píng</rt></ruby>　　　<ruby>纸箱<rt>zhǐ xiāng</rt></ruby>

<ruby>空罐子<rt>guàn</rt></ruby>　　　<ruby>报纸<rt>bào zhǐ</rt></ruby>

<ruby>塑料袋<rt>sù liào dài</rt></ruby>　　　<ruby>杂志<rt>zá zhì</rt></ruby>

　　　<ruby>纸<rt>zhǐ</rt></ruby>

小世界

烤肉很麻烦
má fán

　　我爸爸、妈妈喜欢请朋友到家里吃烤肉，他们说吃烤肉很自在，不拘束，jū shù hái小孩也可以一边吃一边玩儿。我虽然喜欢吃烤肉，但是家里烤肉时，我要帮忙准备东西，还要帮忙收拾东西，我实在shí不喜欢。我觉得请朋友到家里吃烤肉太麻烦了。má fán

应该多烤肉

　　我爸爸常请朋友到家里吃饭，每次妈妈和我都在厨房里准备饭菜，忙得chú de不得了。我想，如果客人到我们家吃dé liǎo烤肉的话，妈妈和我就不用在厨房里忙着做菜了。我觉得我们应该多请朋友吃烤肉。

做回收

我觉得现在的人用太多东西了，实在很浪费。我们有很多东西都可以回收再利用。我们家有一个垃圾桶，一个回收桶。我帮忙做回收。我把空瓶子、空罐子和报纸、杂志都放到回收桶里。

不做回收

虽然我们家有回收桶，但是我们觉得做回收太麻烦，太浪费时间了。我们的垃圾很多，我们把回收桶拿来放垃圾。我觉得，家里有两个垃圾桶实在很方便。

2 到公园烤肉

聊天室

1. 你们常烤肉吗？都在哪儿烤肉？

2. 你们烤肉时都准备什么东西？

3. 你喜欢烤肉吗？为什么？

4. 你在家常帮忙收拾东西吗？

5. 哪些东西是可以回收的？你们怎么做回收？

带个盘子去

1

🔺 今天去 Mary 家吃饭，你要带什么去？
⚥ 今天不用带东西，只要带个盘子(pán)去。

2

🔺 带盘子(pán)？她们家没有盘子(pán)吗？
⚥ 大概(gài)是她家里人少，盘子(pán)不多吧！

3

🔺 那么就多带几个盘子(pán)去吧！
⚥ ……

4

🔺 回来了。怎么样？
⚥ 怎么样？真是太丢(diū)人了！

5

⚥ …大家都带了一盘(pán)菜去，就我一个人没带。
🔺 你不是说只要带一个盘子去吗？

6

⚥ 是啊(a)，我记得(jì)她告诉我："Just bring a plate!"

3 Everything is fine（一切都很好）

Listen and discuss -

1. Who did Mr. Huang write to and what are his regards?
2. What is his impression of students here?
3. How does he feel about his host family?
4. Where did he visit recently and what did he do there?
5. What is his plan in the near future?

（三）一切都很好

昨天晚上黄老师写了一封信给他的妻子。

玉红：

时间过得真快，我已经来了快一个月了。这儿一切都很好，请放心。在学校，虽然有几个学生上课不用心，爱捣蛋，但是多半的学生学习都很认真。

小明一家人都对我很好，把我当自己人。他们的家十分宽敞，院子很大，有一个温水游泳池。我现在天天游泳。我觉得他们的环保做得还不错，游泳池是利用太阳能加温的，他们的回收也做得挺好的。

上个星期六我去动物园玩儿，看到了很多澳大利亚特有的动物。我喂了袋鼠，也和考拉一起拍照。听说考拉几乎一生都不喝水。它们看起来懒洋洋的，十分可爱。

春假快到了，我打算利用这个机会到各地走走，体验不同的风土人情。你自己一个人在家，一切小心。

想你！

东星

五月十八日

资料箱

● 他上课用心吗？

他上课很用心。

很用心　　不用心　　<ruby>爱捣蛋<rt>ài dǎo</rt></ruby>　　<ruby>爱发问<rt>wèn</rt></ruby>　　<ruby>爱讲话<rt>jiǎng</rt></ruby>　　<ruby>常打瞌睡<rt>kē shuì</rt></ruby>

● 我们应该怎么做环保？

我们应该多利用太阳能。

多利用太<ruby>阳<rt>yáng</rt></ruby>能

多做回收

不<ruby>浪费<rt>làng fèi</rt></ruby>水

不浪费电

保<ruby>护<rt>hù</rt></ruby>动物

● 这是什么地方的特有动物？

袋鼠是澳大利亚的特有动物。

<ruby>袋鼠<rt>dài shǔ</rt></ruby>－<ruby>澳<rt>ào</rt></ruby>大利<ruby>亚<rt>yà</rt></ruby>

<ruby>考拉<rt>lā</rt></ruby>－澳大利亚

<ruby>奇异鸟<rt>qí yì niǎo</rt></ruby>－新西兰

<ruby>大熊猫<rt>xióng māo</rt></ruby>－中国

<ruby>老虎<rt>hǔ</rt></ruby>－<ruby>亚洲<rt>yà zhōu</rt></ruby>

<ruby>秃鹰<rt>tū yīng</rt></ruby>－<ruby>北美洲<rt>měi zhōu</rt></ruby>

<ruby>河<rt>hé</rt></ruby>马－非洲

小 世 界

不用心

我们班上课时有的人很用心，常发问^{wèn}，

学习认真；有的人很不用心，爱讲话^{ài jiǎng}，爱

捣蛋^{dǎo}，有时候还打瞌睡^{kē shuì}。

唱^{chàng} 得不错

哥哥喜欢一边洗澡^{xǐ zǎo}一边唱歌^{chàng gē}。

他洗一次澡几乎^{jī hū}要半个小时。妈妈

常骂^{mà}他："洗澡洗那么久，又浪费^{làng fèi}

水，又浪费电。"可是爸爸说他的

歌唱得还不错。

在这儿你一切都好吗？

还好。在这里，我有不少朋友，好吃的东西也很多。我挺^{tǐng}习惯的。

感觉很好

我现在天天做运动，　早上跑步（pǎo bù），傍晚（bàng）游泳。我晴天、雨天都跑步；热天、冷天都游泳。我觉得下雨天跑步的感觉很好，冷天游泳的感觉更棒（bàng）。

做环保

弟弟最近忙得不得了。他每天都拿（ná）很多瓶子（píng）、罐子（guàn）、杂志（zá zhì）和报纸（bào zhǐ）回家。

他昨天带回来了三只猫（māo），今天又带回来了两只狗，都是没人要的。他告诉我们：“老师说我们得做环保。你看，我在做回收，也在保护（hù）动物。”

在这儿你一切都好吗？

一点都不好。我想家，想我的朋友，想我妈妈。我要回家！

聊天室

1. 你班上的同学上课用心吗？

2. 你觉得你学习认真吗？为什么？

3. 你冬天游泳吗？为什么？

4. 你们都怎么做环保？

5. 你喂(wèi)过什么动物？和什么动物一起拍(pāi)过照？

6. 快放暑假了，你打算利用这个机会做什么？

泡好茶

苏东坡(Sū pō)是宋代(Sòng dài)有名的文学(míng wén)家。有一天，他到一座(zuò)寺庙(sì miào)去。

老和尚(shàng)看他穿得不怎么样，就对他不怎么客气，只说："坐"，然后回头对小和尚(shàng)说："茶"。

他们聊了一会儿天以后，老和尚(shàng)觉得这个人还挺(tǐng)有学问(wèn)的，就对他客气了些，说："请坐"，然后回头对小和尚(shàng)说："泡(pào)茶"。

后来，老和尚(shàng)知道他就是有名(míng)的苏东坡(Sū pō)，就

非 常 客 气 地 说：

"请上坐"，然后回头对小和尚说：

"泡(pào)好茶"。

苏东坡(Sū pō)要走时，老和尚请他留(liú)几个字。

苏东坡就写了一副(fù)对联(lián)给他：

坐，请坐，请上坐；

茶，泡茶，泡好茶。

例 句

1　**When in Rome do as the Romans do　入 乡 随 俗**

对　　对 is used in many ways:

(1) **correct, right,** e.g. 对，没错。

(2) **opposite,** e.g. 对面

(3) (对 + O) **to or towards** Used as a preposition, equivalent to 'to or towards' the object following it.

我对这里的印象很好。

妈妈对哥哥的女朋友印象很差。

他们一家人都对我很好。

十分　　**very, extremely**

爸爸今天十分高^{xing}兴。

他这个人十分热心。

多半　　**most, mostly**

我们班的学生多半数学很好。

我的朋友多半看过这部电影。

弟弟上学多半骑自行车。

2　**Barbecue in the park　到 公 园 烤 肉**

一边（儿）……一边（儿）……　**do one thing while doing another**

他们常一边吃饭一边看电视。

弟弟喜欢一边玩电脑一边听音乐。

有的……有的……　**some... while some...**

下课后有的人要去逛^{guàng jiē}街，有的人要去看电影。

这些^{píng guǒ}苹果有的很^{tián}甜，有的不甜。

2

自在　　**at ease, comfortable**

在这儿，我觉得很自在，一点都不拘束（jū shù）。

她怎么了，看起来很不自在？

在他们家，我觉得很不自在。

……以后／以前　**after / before ...**　The 以 can be omitted and use 后／前 only.

功课做好以后，他就出去（chū）玩了。

客人来以前要先把东西准备好。

3　**Everything is fine　一 切 都 很 好**

一切　[yíqiè] **everything, all**

家里一切都很好，请放心。

住在他家，我一切都不习惯。

自己人　**one of us, one of the members**　Used to indicate a close relation.

大家都是自己人，不要客气。

这家人对我很好，把我当自己人。

几乎　[jīhū]　(1)　几乎（hū）**almost**

他几乎每天都很晚才回家。

她几乎和她妈妈一样高了。

(2)　几乎不／没 **hardly**

他今天不舒服，几乎什么东西都没吃。

她昨天晚上几乎没睡（shuì）觉。

V + 到　When used after a verb, "到" indicates the outcome of an action.

我昨天见到了新来的汉语老师。

弟弟找不到他的数学作业。

生 词

1 When in Rome do as the Romans do　入 乡 随 俗

有朋自远方来	yǒu péng zì yuǎnfāng lái	a friend from afar　朋 - friend; 自 - from; self
远方	yuǎnfāng	*n.* distant place　远 - far; 方 - square, direction
入乡随俗	rù xiāng suí sú	*idiom.* when in Rome do as the Romans do　入 - to enter; 乡 - country, village; 随 - to follow; 俗 - custom
学期	xuéqī	*n.* term, semester
交换	jiāohuàn	*v.* exchange, swap　交 - to cross, to interact; 换 - to exchange
打招呼	dǎ zhāohu	*v.* greet somebody　招呼 - say hello to
无所不谈	wú suǒ bù tán	*idiom.* chat freely　无 - nothing, nil
各地	gèdì	*adv.* every region　各 - each, every; 地 - land, floor, ground
印象	yìnxiàng	*n.* impression　印 - to print, seal; 象 - appearance; elephant
友善	yǒushàn	*adj.* friendly　友 - friend; 善 - good, kind
空气	kōngqì	*n.* air　（天）空 - [kōng] sky; [kòng] spare time
新鲜	xīnxiān	*adj.* fresh　新 - new; 鲜 - fresh
气候	qìhòu	*n.* climate　气 - air; 候 - time
宜人	yírén	*adj.* pleasant, delightful　宜 - suitable
交通	jiāotōng	*n.* traffic　交 - to cross; 通 - to get through
让	ràng	*n.* give way; let, allow
行人	xíngrén	*n.* pedestrian　行 - to go, OK
深	shēn	*adj.* deep, dark
风景	fēngjǐng	*n.* scenery　风 - wind; 景 - view, scene
十分	shífēn	*adv.* very, fully, extremely
优美	yōuměi	*adj.* fine, exquisite　优 - outstanding; 美 - beautiful
名胜	míngshèng	*n.* well-known scenic spot
古迹	gǔjì	*n.* historic site　古 - ancient; 迹 - trace
小吃	xiǎochī	*n.* snack
世界	shìjiè	*n.* world　世 - world; 界 - boundary
体验	tǐyàn	*v.* experience　体 - body; 验 - to examine
不同	bùtóng	*adj.* different　同 - same
风土人情	fēngtǔ rénqíng	local conditions and customs　风 - wind; 土 - earth; 人 - people; 情 - feelings
各种	gèzhǒng	*n.* various kinds　各 - each, every; 种 - kind, type
习惯	xíguàn	*v.* get used to　习 - to practise; 惯 - to get used to
西方	xīfāng	*n.* the West（the East - 东方）
以前	yǐqián	*adv.* before, formerly, previously
旅行团	lǚxíngtuán	*n.* tourist group　团 - group
多半	duōbàn	*adv.* mostly
闯	chuǎng	*v.* rush, force one's way in or out
堵车	dǔchē	*v.* have a traffic jam　堵 - to block up; 车 - vehicle
好客	hàokè	*adj.* be hospitable　好 [hào] - like, love; 客（人）- guest
机会	jīhuì	*n.* chance, opportunity
普通话	pǔtōnghuà	*n.* Mandarin, literally common speech　普通 - common

2

| 随便 | suíbiàn | *adj.* easy going, not fussy |
| 饱 | bǎo | *adj.* be full |

2 Barbecue in the park　到公园烤肉

公园	gōngyuán	*n.* park　公 - public; 园 - garden
烤肉	kǎoròu	*v. & n.* barbecue　烤 - to grill, to toast; 肉 - meat
父母亲	fùmǔqīn	*n.* parents　父亲 - father; 母亲 - mother
希望	xīwàng	*v.* hope　希 - to hope; 望 - to expect
附近	fùjìn	*adj.* nearby, in the vicinity
香肠	xiāngcháng	*n.* sausage　香 - fragrant, nice-smelling; 肠 - intestine
牛排	niúpái	*n.* steak　牛 - cow, ox; 排 - row, line
肉串	ròuchuàn	*n.* kebab　肉 - meat; 串 - a string of
面包	miànbāo	*n.* bread　面 - wheat flour; 包 - to wrap
沙拉	shālā	*n.* salad [transliteration]
咖啡	kāfēi	*n.* coffee [transliteration]
可乐	kělè	*n.* cola [transliteration]
啤酒	píjiǔ	*n.* beer　啤 - [transliteration]; 酒 - alcoholic drink
一边 … …	yìbiān...yìbiān...	do one thing while doing another, e.g.
一边 … …		一边吃饭一边看电视 - watch TV while eating
有的	yǒude	*adj.* some, a few
感觉	gǎnjué	*n.* feeling; *v.* feel　感 - to feel, sense; 觉 - to feel
自在	zìzai	*adj.* at ease, comfortable
拘束	jūshù	*v.* restrict, restrain　拘 - to detain; 束 - to tie
实在	shízài	*adv.* really　实 - real, fact
收拾	shōushi	*v.* tidy up, put in order　收 - to collect, to receive; 拾 - to pick up
垃圾	lājī	*n.* rubbish, garbage, pronounced as lèsè in Taiwan
丢	diū	*v.* throw, lose
桶	tǒng	*n.* bin, bucket, barrel
空	kōng	*adj.* empty; [kòng] free time
瓶子	píngzi	*n.* bottle, vase　瓶 - bottle, vase; 子 - [zi] suffix for some common nouns with one character, [zǐ] son
罐子	guànzi	*n.* tin, can, jar
塑料袋	sùliàodài	*n.* plastic bag　塑料 - plastic; 袋 - bag
回收	huíshōu	*v.* recycle　回 - to return; 收 - to collect
心里	xīnli	in (one's) heart
重视	zhòngshì	*v.* consider important　重 - heavy; 视 - sight
环保	huánbǎo	*n.* environmental protection　环 (境 jìng)- environment; 保 (护 hù) - protection; 环 - ring, to surround; 保 - to keep
火锅	huǒguō	*n.* hot pot　火 - fire; 锅 - pot, wok
包	bāo	*v.* to wrap
饮茶	yǐnchá	*n.* yum cha - a Cantonese meal of small snacks and tea
纸箱	zhǐxiāng	*n.* carton　纸 - paper; 箱 - box
报纸	bàozhǐ	*n.* newspaper　报 - to report; 纸 - paper
杂志	zázhì	*n.* magazine　杂 - miscellaneous; 志 - records
纸	zhǐ	*n.* paper

麻烦	máfan	*adj.* troublesome, inconvenient
小孩	xiǎohái	*n.* children
应该	yīnggāi	*v.* should, ought to

3　Everything is fine　一切都很好

一切	yíqiè	*n.* everything, all　切 - to cut
妻子	qīzi	*n.* wife (formal term)
玉红	Yùhóng	*n.* a woman's name　玉 - jade; 红 - red
用心	yòngxīn	*adj.* attentive, diligent　用 - to use; 心 - heart
捣蛋	dǎodàn	*v.* make trouble　捣 - to smash; 蛋 - egg
当	dàng	*v.* treat as, regard as; [dāng] be, work as, serve as
自己人	zìjǐrén	*n.* one of us, people on one's own side
宽敞	kuānchang	*adj.* spacious, roomy　宽 - wide, broad; 敞 - open
院子	yuànzi	*n.* courtyard
温水游泳池	wēnshuǐ yóuyǒngchí	*n.* heated pool　温 - warm; 水 - water
太阳能	tàiyángnéng	*n.* solar energy　太阳 - sun; 能 - energy, to be able to
加温	jiāwēn	*v.* heat　加 - to add; 温 - warm
动物园	dòngwùyuán	*n.* zoo　动物 - animal; 园 - garden
特有	tèyǒu	*adj.* peculiar　特 - special
喂	wèi	*v.* feed; *int.* hello
袋鼠	dàishǔ	*n.* kangaroo　袋 - bag; 鼠 - mouse, rat
考拉	kǎolā	*n.* koala [transliteration], also called 树熊 shùxióng or 无尾熊 wúwěixióng　无 - no, without; 尾 - tail; 熊 - bear
几乎	jīhū	*adv.* almost　几 - [jī] nearly; [jǐ] how many, a few
一生	yìshēng	*n.* all one's life
懒洋洋	lǎnyángyáng	*adj.* sluggish, listless　懒 - lazy; 洋 - vast, ocean
春假	chūnjià	*n.* spring holiday　春 - spring; 假 - holiday
走走	zǒuzou	*v.* travel around, walk around
小心	xiǎoxīn	*v.* be careful, take care　心 - heart
发问	fāwèn	*v.* ask or raise a question　发 - [fā] to send, [fà] hair; 问 - ask
讲话	jiǎnghuà	*v.* talk, speak
打瞌睡	dǎ kēshuì	*v.* doze off
保护	bǎohù	*v.* protect; *n.* protection　保 - to keep; 护 - to protect
奇异鸟	qíyìniǎo	*n.* kiwi bird　奇异 - fantastic, bizarre
大熊猫	dàxióngmāo	*n.* giant panda
亚洲	Yàzhōu	*n.* Asia　洲 - continent
秃鹰	tūyīng	*n.* bald eagle　秃 - bald; 鹰 - eagle
北美洲	Běi Měizhōu	*n.* North America　洲 - continent
河马	hémǎ	*n.* hippopotamus　河 - river
非洲	Fēizhōu	*n.* Africa　洲 - continent
有时侯	yǒushíhou	*adv.* sometimes
洗澡	xǐzǎo	*v.* take a bath　洗 - to wash; 澡 - bath
傍晚	bàngwǎn	*n.* dusk, early evening　傍 - to be close to; 晚 - evening
棒	bàng	*adj.* [oral] excellent, good
每天	měitiān	*n.* everyday

2

学写字

Radical in color

位 wèi *[m.w. for person]*	各 gè *every, each*	印 yìn *to print; seal*	象 xiàng *appearance; elephant*	告 gào *inform*
诉 sù *tell; appeal to*	通 tōng *to get through*	世 shì *world*	界 jiè *boundary*	种 zhǒng *kind, type*
惯 guàn *to get used to*	园 yuán *garden*	烤 kǎo *to grill, to toast, to bake*	肉 ròu *meat*	父 fù *father*
母 mǔ *mother*	亲 qīn *related by blood*	希 xī *to hope*	望 wàng *to expect*	牛 niú *ox, cow*
拾 shí *to pick up*	它 tā *it*	环 huán *to surround; ring, hoop*	保 bǎo *to keep*	切 qiè *to cut*
封 fēng *[m.w. for letter]*	游 yóu *to swim; to play*	泳 yǒng *swim*	特 tè *special*	护 hù *to protect*

2

文化厅

❀ Confucius

Confucius, 孔子 Kǒng Zǐ (551~479 BC), was a great philosopher and educator. He was born in 春秋时期, the Spring and Autumn Periods, when China was under the reign of many individual states. Politics and trickery were played by the rulers and society showed apparent unease. Witnessing the decline of morality, 孔子 stood to advocate righteousness in politics, and in society. He toured around the states seeking political influence but gained little success.

Confucius (551~479 B.C.), great philosopher and educator

The greatest successes of 孔子 were in literature and education. Based on the history of his home state 鲁 lǔ, he wrote the classic 春秋 Chūnqiū. It became an important Chinese historical document, and earned the name 春秋时期 for that period. His teaching career started in his late 20s and continued throughout his life. He tutored privately and took pupils regardless of their social and financial status. Many of them followed him around for long periods of time. He was said to have as many as three thousand disciples.

Confucius with his disciples

孔子 taught through discussions, drawing from personal experiences and ancient documents. Soon after his death, his numerous dialogues with his disciples were compiled into 论语 Lúnyǔ, *The Analects of Confucius*. The doctrines in the book have since influenced the lives and thoughts of the Chinese people. Today, Confucius' sayings are still quoted respectfully by the Chinese in their daily lives.

有朋自远方来，不亦乐乎？
（论语 1-1）

Isn't it also a pleasure when friends come from afar?

父母在，不远游；游必有方。
（论语 4-19）

Do not travel far when parents are alive and travel only where planned.

非礼勿视，非礼勿听，非礼勿言，非礼勿动。
（论语 12-1）

See no evil, hear no evil, speak no evil and do no evil.

Not only revered as a teacher, 孔子 was treated like a father by his disciples. After his death, many of them held three years of mourning for him. A pupil 子贡 Zǐgòng built a hut in front of his tomb and mourned there for six years. Chinese people later built temples, 孔庙 kǒngmiào, to honor and worship him. Today, Chinese people still hold ceremonies with classic dances on his birthday 九月二十八日 at the 孔庙 of many large cities. Parents will take their children to 孔庙 to be blessed, wishing that they study well.

孔庙 kǒng miào, *temple of Confucius*

✿ Local food variety

The Chinese consider themselves consumers of a great variety of foods; a variety originating not from different countries but from different regions within China. Because China covers a vast area that ranges from subtropical to cold climates, each region has developed its own local flavor. 南甜北咸，东辣西酸 nántián běixián, dōnglà xīsuān used to be an expression to describe the typical local differences, that is, sweet in the south, salty in the north, spicy hot in the east and sour in the west. Although these differences have decreased due to improvements in transportation

四川 Sìchuān *food is noted for its hot and spicy flavour.*

and communication between regions, there are still some dishes that carry a typical local flavor. Those originating from southern regions such as 广东 Guǎngdōng tend to have a sweet flavor. Typical dishes are sweet and sour pork and lemon chicken. Yum cha, the popular snack food, also originated from 广东. Those originating from 四川 Sìchuān and 湖南 Húnán tend to have a spicy hot flavor. Typical dishes are 麻婆豆腐 mápó dòufu, spicy fried chicken 麻辣子鸡 málà zǐjī and 宫保鸡丁 gōngbǎo jīdīng. The Beijing region is famous for its snack dishes, such as 饺子 and Peking duck 北京烤鸭 Běijīng kǎoyā. Dishes originating from Taiwan generally have a salty flavor. Taiwan is also famous for its snack foods such as smelly bean curd 臭豆腐 chòu dòufu and oyster pancake 蚵仔煎, pronounced as e'ājiān in Taiwanese.

臭豆腐 chòu dòufu *is a dish detested by some but loved by others.*

❀ Expressions using '吃' or '喝'

吃得开 – describes a person who is able to perform well.

他很会说话，到哪里都很吃得开。

He is a sweet talker and is popular everywhere he goes.

吃醋 – jealous, 醋 cù means vinegar.

我一和别的男孩子说话，我的男朋友就吃醋。

My boyfriend gets jealous whenever I talk to other boys.

喝西北风 – drink the north-western wind.

他没钱请女朋友看电影，只好带她去喝西北风。

He doesn't have money to take his girlfriend to the cinema and can only take her to drink the cold winter wind.

吃错药了 – describes a person who behaves abnormally.

你今天怎么对我这么好？吃错药了？

Why are you so nice to me today? Have you taken the wrong medication?

吃豆腐 – 1. to eat beancurd; 2. to flirt with women, used colloquially to describe men making advances towards women without serious intentions.

他很喜欢吃豆腐。

He likes eating beancurd.

他很喜欢吃女孩子的豆腐。

He likes to flirt with and make advances towards girls.

❀ **Chinese food vs Western food**

Traditionally, the three daily meals Chinese people have are quite different from that of Westerners. Although the difference has become less obvious in some urban areas, distinct customs are still prevalent in rural areas. Listed here is a comparison between what a typical Chinese and a typical Westerner would have for their meals:

	中国人	西方人
早餐	馒头 mántou steamed bun　　稀饭 xīfàn rice porridge　　小菜 pickles 包子　　豆浆 dòujiāng soya milk 烧饼油条 shāobǐng yóutiáo sesame seed cake and fried stick	土司 tǔsī toast　　麦片粥 màipiànzhōu porridge 谷类食品 gǔ lèi shípǐn cereal　　面包 培根和煎蛋 péigēn hé jiāndàn bacon and eggs　　水果 茶　　咖啡 kāfēi　　牛奶 niúnǎi
午餐	汤面　　饺子 炒面　　炒饭	三明治 sānmíngzhì　　热狗 烤肉饼 kǎoròubǐng meat pie 果汁　　汽水　　汉堡包　　沙拉 shālā
晚餐	米饭　　鱼 yú　　肉 蔬菜 shūcài vegetable　　汤	烤鸡 kǎojī barbecue chicken　　牛排 披萨 pīsà pizza 炖羊肉 dùnyángròu lamb stew　　意大利面 pasta

2

第三课 挣零花钱
zhèng líng huā

1 Feeling great（感觉真好）

Listen and discuss -

1. What has become popular in the class lately and why?
2. What jobs are available?
3. What job does Xiaoming have? What are the working hours?
4. How does Xiaoming get to and from work?
5. How does Xiaoming feel about having a part-time job?

（一）感觉真好

最近，我们班上正在流行打工。大家都在工作，挣零花钱。

同学们有时候会一起去看电影，打保龄球，或逛街买东西。每次出去玩儿都要花钱。如果我们能自己打工挣零花钱，就不用老是跟父母亲要钱了。

打工的机会挺多的：快餐店常招服务员，书店常招店员，地方报纸也常招送报员；有的工资不高，但是有的也还不错。

我在快餐店找到一份工作，每个星期做十二个小时，工资还可以。工作时间是星期一、三、五下午三点半到七点半。我放学后走路到店里工作，下班时姐姐接我回家。

有时候，我回到家里累得半死，什么事都不想做。不过，我觉得虽然工作很累，但是回报还不错。昨天妈妈刚好没钱，我就给了她五十块。妈妈很高兴，给了我一个拥吻。当时的感觉真好！

资料箱

● 你为什么打工？

因为我想挣零花钱。

想挣零花钱

想帮父母挣钱

想有工作经验

在家无聊

觉得好玩儿

● 你打什么工？

我当送报员。

在快餐店当服务员

在咖啡馆当服务员

在饭馆当服务员

在书店当店员

在唱片行当店员

在水果店当店员

当送报员

当家教

● 他们在招什么？

招店员

书店招店员
十五岁 ~ 二十六岁，会说普通话

时间：　星期四下午五时 ~ 八时
　　　　星期六上午九时 ~ 下午三时

工资：　每小时十七元

电话：　9876 5432

家教

招家教，教九年级数学和科学。

时间：　星期三下午七时 ~ 九时
　　　　星期日上午十时 ~ 十一时

工资：　每小时二十五元。

住址：　长和路 １２３号

小 世 界

打工挣钱

　　去年暑假我打了工，今年暑假我想再去打工。虽然打工很累，可是回报还不错。我喜欢和同学去看电影和逛街 guàng jiē 买东西。自己打工挣了钱，就不用老是跟父母亲要零花钱了。

工作机会少

　　我想打工，可是不知道要打什么工。在书店当店员实在 shí wú 无聊，当送报员也很没意思，在快餐店当服务 wù 员又会累得半 sǐ 死。我觉得好的工作机会实在很少。

不打工

我没打过工。我觉得打工一点都不好玩儿，天天累得半死（sǐ），挣的钱也不多。我父母亲也说打工太浪（làng）

费（fèi）时间了，他们不要我打工。他们平常都给我不少零花钱，让我和同学去看电影、逛街（guàng jiē）或喝咖啡（kā fēi），所以我就不打工了。

没时间打工

我今年加入（rù）了交响（xiǎng）乐团（tuán），每天要练（liàn）一个小时的小提琴（tí qín）；下个星期要参加科学比赛，现在正在忙着学习；明年要去北京当交换（huàn）学生，也得利用时间好好儿练习（liàn pǔ）普通话。我实（shí）在太忙了，没时间打工。

聊天室

1. 你打过工吗？为什么打工？

2. 你喜欢打什么工？为什么？

3. 你的朋友打工吗？多半在哪儿工作？

4. 你觉得什么时间打工最好？为什么？

5. 你觉得打工的回报怎么样？

6. 在六十一页的两份工作，你会选哪个？为什么？

挣来的

1

我们星期六去看电影，怎么样？

不行，我没钱看电影。

2

你打工的钱呢？

都给了我父母亲了。

3

你真是好孩子。你一个星期有多少零花钱？

我有五块钱。你呢？

4

我父母没给我零花钱，我的钱都是挣来的。

你没有打工，怎么挣钱？

5

我妈妈说，我如果吃了早饭再上学，她那天就给我二十块。……

6

……我这个星期有三天吃了早饭，一共挣了六十块。

2 Really unbearable（真受不了 shòu liǎo）

Listen and discuss -

1. Who of Dawei's friends are working? And where do they work?
2. How does Lanlan like her job?
3. How are Li Qiu's working conditions?
4. What was Dawei's work experience?
5. Do you think Lanlan will quit her job? Justify your answer.

（二）真受不了

🗣 大伟，最近很多人在打工，你知道吗？

🗣 我知道。小明在快餐店工作，李秋在咖啡馆当服务员。听说你也在餐馆工作。那儿的工作环境怎么样？

🗣 不太好。顾客多半吸烟，里面到处都是烟味，我很受不了。

🗣 听说李秋的工作不错，是吗？

🗣 是啊！那家咖啡馆不让吸烟，所以她不用吸二手烟。她的老板很照顾员工，顾客的态度也很好。还有，她的工资也高。

🗣 李秋的运气真好，我的运气就差多了。去年我曾经在一家杂货店打工，那儿不但工资低，而且工作环境也差。

🗣 真的啊？

🗣 是啊！店里又脏又乱，顾客水平也差。他们常把东西藏起来不付钱，或把东西用坏了再拿回去退钱。

🗣 我的天，那真让人受不了。

🗣 还有，我的老板凶得不得了，一天到晚发脾气，所以我做了两个星期就把工作辞了。

🗣 那种工作辞了也好。我也想把我的工作辞了，不过因为工资不错，辞了有点儿可惜。

资 料 箱

🔘 这儿的工作环境怎么样？

这儿老板很照顾员工。

老板人很好

老板人很客气

老板很照顾员工

老板凶得不得了
（xiōng）（liǎo）

顾客态度很好
（gù）（tài dù）

顾客态度很差

顾客多半吸烟
（xī yān）

又脏又乱
（zāng luàn）

🔘 你为什么把工作辞了？
（cí）

因为我做得太累了。

老板很凶
（bǎn）（xiōng）

顾客的态度很差
（gù）（tài dù）

工作环境很差

工资太低了
（zī）（dī）

我做得太累了

我功课太忙了

🔘 什么事最让你受不了？

我最受不了的是
老板发脾气。

老板发脾气
（bǎn）

顾客态度差
（gù）（tài dù）

老师太凶
（xiōng）

考试太多

作业太多

空气太差
（kōng）

电脑死机
（sǐ）

吸二手烟
（xī）（yān）

小世界

二手烟
yān

我最讨厌二手烟了，一吸到二手烟我就咳嗽。平常去餐馆吃饭，或去咖啡馆喝咖啡的时候，常有顾客吸烟，里面到处都是烟味，真让人受不了。

不让吸烟
xī yān

我以前常吸二手烟，现在不了。以前很多地方像火车站、餐馆、办公室等，都让吸烟，所以常要吸二手烟。现在很多地方都不让吸烟了，所以二手烟就少多了。

受不了
liǎo

我妈妈一天到晚发脾气，我们都很受不了。我爸爸的脾气好得不得了，我们也很受不了。

运气不错

　　我觉得我的运气还不错。这份工作工资^{zī}高，工作

^{qīng sōng}轻松，老板人很客气，顾^{gù}客的态度^{tài dù}也很好。

倒霉极了 ^{dǎo méi jí}

　　我哪来的运气？我倒霉极了^{dǎo méi jí}！这

儿的工作环境差，顾^{gù}客的态度^{tài dù}也差，

老板又凶得不得了^{bǎn xiōng} ^{liǎo}，一天到晚发脾气。

我天天回到家都累得半死^{sǐ}。

辞了可惜 ^{cí} ^{xī}

　　虽然我不喜欢那份工作，但是那份工

作很轻松^{qīng sōng}，工资^{zī}也不错，辞了很可惜^{cí} ^{xī}。而且，

如果我把工作辞了，我就没有钱请你喝咖^{kā}

啡^{fēi}了。

聊天室

1. 你喜欢什么样的工作环境？

2. 你吸(xī)过二手烟(yān)吗？感觉怎么样？

3. 你常发脾气吗？为什么？

4. 如果你的老板(bǎn)很凶(xiōng)，你怎么办(bàn)？

5. 你看到过态度(tài dù)差的顾(gù)客吗？当时的感觉怎么样？

6. 什么事最让你受不了(liǎo)？

退钱

😊 对不起，我有东西要退(tuì)钱。

1

😣 有收据(jù)吗？

😊 有，都在这儿。

2

😣 好吧！你要退(tuì)什么东西？

😊 我要退(tuì)这些……

3

😊 这件衬衫(chèn shān)现在太小了。

4

😊 这条裤子(tiáo kù)现在太短了。

5

😊 这顶帽子(dǐng mào)不太好看。

6

😊 这双鞋(shuāng xié)……太旧(jiù)了。

7

3 A long hesitation（犹豫了半天）

Listen and discuss -

1. How does Xiaoming manage his part-time work earnings?
2. What did Xiaoming decide to buy and why did he make such a choice?
3. When did he go shopping and who did he go with?
4. What shop attracted them and why?
5. What was the decision Xiaoming had to make that day?
6. Describe Xiaoming's decision-making process. What are the pros and cons?

（三）犹^{yóu}豫^{yù}了半天

从^{cóng}我开始^{shǐ}打工到现在已经一个多月了。挣来的钱，除了零花以外，我都把它存^{cún}起来。现在我已经存了一百多块钱了。我打算用这些钱去买个随身^{suí shēn}听，因为妈妈常唠叨^{láo dāo}，说我把音乐开得太大声^{shēng}、太吵^{chǎo}。如果有随身听，我就不用担^{dān}心吵到别人了。

星期五下课后，我和几个同学一起去逛街^{guàng jiē}。有一家流行服饰^{shì}店把音乐开得很大声^{shēng}，我们一边听音乐，一边就走了进^{jìn}去。这家服饰^{shì}店卖的都是名牌^{míng pái}衣服，价^{jià}钱都很贵。我试穿了一件上衣和一条裤^{tiáo kù}子，觉得还挺^{tǐng}不错的。同学们也都说我看起来很酷^{kù}。我很动心，可是又有点儿犹^{yóu}豫^{yù}。买这么贵的衣服，妈妈一定^{dìng}会唠叨半天；而且，买了衣服，就没钱买随身^{suí shēn}听了。不过，这衣服料^{liào}子好，式^{shì}样又流行，我实^{shí}在很喜欢，同学们也一直怂恿^{zhí sǒng yǒng}我买。

犹^{yóu}豫^{yù}了半天，最后我选择^{xuǎn zé}了买衣服。随身听只好等以后再买了，妈妈要唠叨也就让她唠叨了。

资 料 箱

如果你存了钱，你最想做什么？

我想买一个随身听。

买一个随身听

买一部电脑

买一辆车

买名牌衣服

买游戏光盘

去中国旅行

存更多钱

你买衣服都怎么选择？

我选名牌的。

名牌的

式样流行的

颜色好看的

料子好的

看起来很酷的

穿起来舒服的

便宜的

他的父母常唠叨些什么？

他们常唠叨他把音乐开得太大声。

把音乐开得太大声

房间太乱

花太多钱

学习不认真

整天看电视

睡觉太晚

早上起不来

一天到晚往外跑

车开得太快

小 世 界

存钱
^{cún}

高美花没打工。她在家帮忙做家事，她妈妈一天

给她五块钱。除了零花以外，她把钱都存起来。
^{cún}

林明存常打工，可是他不存钱。他把挣来
^{Lín}

的钱都拿去看电影和买东西。他说，存
^{ná}

一点儿钱也买不到什么好东西，所以就

不存了。

名牌衣服

张爱宜喜欢买名牌衣服。她觉得名牌衣服
^{ài}

料子好，式样流行，穿起来很舒服，看起来也
^{liào}　^{shì}

很酷。她看到名牌衣服就动心。
^{kù}

白喜名什么衣服都买，

名牌的她买，不是名牌的

她也买。她说，只要是便宜的，看起来好看的，她

就买。

犹豫 (yóu yù)

王西东(Wáng)喜欢穿名牌衣服，可是他一买名牌衣服他妈妈就唠叨。她妈妈说王西东买一件衣服的钱，她可以在菜市场(shì)买三件。所以，王西东每次买名牌衣服，都是同学们一直怂恿(sǒng yǒng)，还犹豫(yóu yù)半天，最后才买下来。

唠叨

黄南觉得他父母亲虽然有点唠叨，但是多半都还好。他说："他们唠叨时，也都是我不对。所以他们唠叨我就让他们唠叨了。"

陈北(Chén)觉得他父母亲太唠叨了。他说：

"他们什么都唠叨：回家晚了啦(la)，玩电子游戏(xì)啦，房间太乱(luàn)啦，作业忘了做啦，考试考不好啦…。他们啊，真是唠叨得不得了。"

聊天室

1. 如果你存了钱，你最想做什么？
^{cún}

2. 你喜欢随身听吗？为什么？
^{suí shēn}

3. 你逛街时，什么东西最让你动心？
^{guàng jiē}

4. 你买名牌衣服吗？为什么？

5. 你父母常唠叨吗？都唠叨些什么？

回家打电话

例 句

1　Feeling great　感觉真好

流行　**popular, in fashion**

　　这个式样的鞋现在很流行。

　　今年很流行红色的衣服。

如果　**if, in case, in the event of**　"如果" is often followed by "就".

　　如果下午不下雨，我们就去游泳。

　　如果太贵的话，就不要买。

老是　**always**　It is usually used when things are unwelcome.

　　他怎么老是忘了带作业？

　　你为什么上课老是迟到？

跟　　(1)　**towards, with (someone/something)**　It introduces the relevant target of an action.

　　他又跟姐姐吵架了。

　　这件事你最好不要跟老师说。

　　(2)　**and, with**

　　我弟弟跟我都喜欢打网球。

　　明天你跟我一块儿去吧。

2　Really unbearable　真受不了

受不了 **cannot endure, unbearable, intolerable**

　　这儿都是烟味，我受不了。

　　他老是迟到，真让人受不了。

3

例 句

到处 **everywhere**

这个公园里到处(chù)都是人。

姐姐的房间里到处都是衣服。

不但……而且…… **not only... but also** Sometimes 不但 is omitted and only 而且 is used.

这儿不但老板(bǎn)人好，而且顾(gù)客的态(tài)度(dù)也好。

她不但人缘(yuán)儿好，而且学习也好。

这件衣服不但好看，而且也很便宜。

v + 起来 (1) **indicate an upward action**

请大家站起来。

(2) **indicate a put-away, put-aside action**

弟弟把巧(qiǎo)克(kè)力(lì)藏(cáng)起来了。

把那本书藏(cáng)起来，别让老师看到。

(3) **express an impression or opinion**

那件旗(qí)袍(páo)她穿起来很好看。

他今天看起来不太高兴(xìng)。

也好 **may as well, may not be a bad idea**

下午没事，去逛(guàng)逛街(jiē)也好。

雨下得这么大，我看你不去也好。

可惜 **it's a pity**

大家都要去看电影，只可惜(xī)我不能去。

我觉得你把那份工作辞(cí)了很可惜。

3　A long hesitation　犹 豫 了 半 天

唠叨 [láodao] **to nag**

> 我妈妈常唠叨，说我的房间太乱。
>
> 好了，我知道了，别再唠叨了。

动心　**heart set on something, be tempted**

> 店里那条连衣裙很好看，我实在很动心。
>
> 朋友找他一起去中国旅行，他很动心。

一直　(1) **continuously**

> 今天上数学课时，她一直在说话。
>
> 你知道吗？对面那个人一直看着你。

　　　(2) **straight (in one direction)**

> 从这条路一直往前走就到我家。

只好　**have no choice but to, have to**

> 我没有零花钱了，只好向姐姐借。
>
> 我今天没赶上车，只好走路回家。

3

生 词

1　Feeling great　感 觉 真 好

挣	zhèng	*v.* earn
零花钱	línghuāqián	*n.* pocket money　零 - small amount, zero; 花 - to spend, flower
流行	liúxíng	*adj.* popular, in fashion　流 - to flow; 行 - to walk, to travel
打工	dǎgōng	*v.* have a part-time job　打 - to hit; 工 - work, job
保龄球	bǎolíngqiú	*n.* bowling (tenpin) [transliteration]
或	huò	*conj.* or, either or
花	huā	*v.* spend, e.g. 花钱 - to spend money; *n.* flower

生词

老是	lǎoshì	*adv.* always, all the time
跟	gēn	*prep.* towards or with, e.g. 跟父母要钱
		conj. and, e.g. 他跟我是好朋友。
快餐	kuàicān	*n.* fast food, e.g. 快餐店 - fast food restaurant
店	diàn	*n.* shop, store
招	zhāo	*v.* recruit
服务员	fúwùyuán	*n.* attendant　服务 - give service to; 员 - personnel
店员	diànyuán	*n.* clerk, salesperson　店 - shop, store; 员 - personnel
地方	dìfāng	*adj.* local; *n.* place, location
送报员	sòngbàoyuán	*n.* newsboy　送 - to deliver; 报 - newspaper; 员 - personnel
工资	gōngzī	*n.* salary, wage　工 - work, job; 资 - capital fund
份	fèn	*m.w.* [for work, newspaper, magazine etc.]
累	lèi	*adj.* tired, fatigued
半死	bànsǐ	*adj.* half dead　半 - half; 死 - dead, to die
回报	huíbào	*n.* return, reward　回 - return; 报 - *v.* to report, *n.* newspaper
刚好	gānghǎo	*adv.* just, so happen that　刚 - just now
拥吻	yōngwěn	*n.* hug and kiss　拥 - hug, to hug; 吻 - kiss, to kiss
当时	dāngshí	*adv.* at that time, then　当 - at the time; to serve, to be
经验	jīngyàn	*n.* experience　经 - to go through; 验 - to examine
唱片行	chàngpiànháng	*n.* music store　唱片 - disk; 行 [háng] - business firm
家教	jiājiào	*n.* private tutor　家 - family, home; 教 - to teach

2　Really unbearable　真受不了

受不了	shòu bù liǎo	*colloq.* cannot endure, unbearable, intolerable
餐馆	cānguǎn	*n.* restaurant　餐 - meal; 馆 - building, shop
工作	gōngzuò	*n.* work, job; *v.* to work
环境	huánjìng	*n.* environment　环 - to surround; 境 - area, situation
顾客	gùkè	*n.* customer, client　顾 - to attend to; 客 - guest
吸烟	xīyān	*v.* smoke　吸 - to inhale; 烟 - cigarette, smoke
到处	dàochù	*adv.* everywhere　到 - to go to; 处 - place
烟味	yānwèi	*n.* cigarette smell　烟 - cigarette, smoke; 味 - smell
二手烟	èrshǒuyān	*n.* passive smoking　二手 - second-hand
老板	lǎobǎn	*n.* boss　老 - old; 板 - board
照顾	zhàogù	*v.* take care of, look after　照 - to take care of; 顾 - to attend to
员工	yuángōng	*n.* employee　员 - personnel; 工 - work, job
态度	tàidù	*n.* attitude　态 - attitude; 度 - degree
运气	yùnqì	*n.* luck　运 - luck, to transport; 气 - air
曾经	céngjīng	*adv.* once, formerly　曾 - once, formerly; 经 - to go through
杂货店	záhuòdiàn	*n.* grocery store　杂 - sundry; 货 - goods
不但	búdàn	*conj.* not only
低	dī	*adj.* low
而且	érqiě	*conj.* also　而 - yet; 且 - also
脏	zāng	*adj.* dirty
乱	luàn	*adj.* messy

3

水平	shuǐpíng	n. standard, level　水 - water; 平 - flat, even
藏	cáng	v. hide
付	fù	v. pay
退	tuì	v. return (things), e.g. 退钱 - to get/give a refund; 退东西 - to return things
我的天	wǒ de tiān	colloq. Oh my God!
脾气	píqi	n. temper, e.g. 发脾气 - to lose temper
辞	cí	v. quit, resign, sack
种	zhǒng	m.w. kind, type
也好	yěhǎo	phr. may as well, may not be a bad idea
可惜	kěxī	it's a pity, too bad　可 - to approve, can; 惜 - to have pity on
死机	sǐjī	v. break down (computer), said as 当机 dàngjī in Taiwan 死 - dead, to die; 机 - machine
轻松	qīngsōng	adj. light and easy　轻 - light; 松 - loose
极	jí	adv. extremely, exceedingly

3　A long hesitation　犹豫了半天

犹豫	yóuyù	v. hesitate, be indecisive
零花	línghuā	v. spend pocket money, e.g. 零花钱 - pocket money
存	cún	v. save, deposit
随身听	suíshēntīng	n. portable listening device, e.g. walkman, ipod, MP3 etc. 随 - to follow; 身 - body; 听 - to listen
唠叨	láodao	v. nag　唠 - talkative; 叨 - talkative
声	shēng	n. sound, voice
吵	chǎo	adj. noisy; v. annoy, quarrel
别人	biérén	n. other people　别 - other, don't
服饰店	fúshìdiàn	n. fashion shop　服 - clothes; 饰 - ornament
进	jìn	v. to enter
名牌	míngpái	n. famous brand　名 - famous, name; 牌 - brand, plate, sign
价钱	jiàqián	n. price　价 - price, value
试穿	shìchuān	v. try on (clothes/shoes)　试 - to try; 穿 - to wear
上衣	shàngyī	n. upper garment　上 - upper, on, to go to; 衣 - clothes
酷	kù	slang cool [transliteration]; cruel, extreme
动心	dòngxīn	adj. heart set on something, be tempted
料子	liàozi	n. material (fabric)
式样	shìyàng	n. style　式 - style; 样 - pattern
一直	yìzhí	adv. continuously　直 - straight
怂恿	sǒngyǒng	v. urge, egg on
选择	xuǎnzé	v. choose; n. option, choice
只好	zhǐhǎo	adv. have to, have no choice but
辆	liàng	m.w. [for bus, car, bicycle, etc.]
颜色	yánsè	n. color　颜 - color; 色 - color
家事	jiāshì	n. housework　事 - business
赶	gǎn	v. catch up with; hurry, rush

3

学写字

Radical in color

流 liú *to flow*	工 gōng *work, job*	挣 zhèng *to earn*	零 líng *small amount; zero*	花 huā *to spend; flower*
或 huò *or, either or*	餐 cān *meal*	店 diàn *shop*	员 yuán *personnel*	报 bào *to report; newspaper*
纸 zhǐ *paper*	份 fèn *[m.w. for job, newspaper]*	累 lèi *tired*	刚 gāng *just now, just*	受 shòu *to bear; to receive*
境 jìng *area, situation*	让 ràng *let, to allow; give way*	曾 céng *once, formerly*	而 ér *yet*	且 qiě *also*
脾 pí *temper*	从 cóng *from, since*	唠 láo *talkative*	叨 dāo *talkative*	进 jìn *to enter*
名 míng *famous; name*	牌 pái *brand; plate, sign*	条 tiáo *strip; measure word*	定 dìng *to set*	直 zhí *straight*

文化厅

🌸 Chinese currency

As in many other ancient civilizations, the Chinese used cowrie shells, 贝 bèi, as a form of currency in early days. Many Chinese characters that relate to value are formed with the radical 贝, such as 贵 and 赛. The traditional form of 买 and 卖 are also in this radical, written as 買 and 賣 (貝 is the traditional form of 贝.)

In addition to 贝, people in 商朝, the Shang Dynasty (11-4th century BC) started using bronze in the shape of 贝. Nuggets in bronze became a common currency not long after. During 770~221 BC currency appeared in different shapes and materials: knife, shell, ring and circle; bronze, gold and silver.

A variety of currency from 770~221B.C. in different shapes and materials.

元宝 yuánbǎo (left) and 铜钱 tóngqián (right)

The complexity in usage of currency was unified by 秦始皇 Qín Shǐhuáng who also unified Chinese writing and measurement. Round coins with a square hole in the middle, with a weight value, became the standard currency. In 621 AD in 唐朝, the Tang Dynasty (618~907 AD), common coins with symbolic value called 通宝 tōngbǎo, or 铜钱 tóngqián, were introduced. These were used by citizens for daily transactions. People strung them into a bunch and tied it to the waistbelt for easy carrying. Another form of currency that carried a much higher value was 元宝 yuánbǎo, the ingot. 元宝 were gold or silver and were traded by weight. They were in various shapes. The best known shape has two high curved ends and is now a symbol of wealth.

As trade became more active, the 唐 businessmen started using paper documents called 飞钱 that act like bank drafts. In 1023 AD in 宋朝, the Song Dynasty, the government officially set up mints to print paper money called 交子 jiāozi. Paper money gradually became popular in 元朝, the Yuan Dynasty. However, 元宝 and 通宝 continued to be the popular currency until the introduction of the Western monetary system in the late Qing Dynasty and early Republic period.

❀ Chinese abacus

When the Chinese say they 'plan' to do something they often use the word 打算 dǎsuàn. The 打 dǎ means to strike or to hit; the 算 suàn comes from 算盘 suànpán, the abacus.

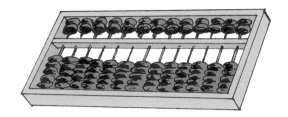

Traditional wooden abacus

There are different theories as to when the Chinese started using the abacus. Some suggest that it was as early as the 1st century. Documents prove that abacuses similar to those used today were in existence in the 12th century. An abacus is made up of rods with beads, with each rod representing a unit of ten. Each rod has two beads on the top section and five beads on the bottom section. Each top bead represents a value of five and each bottom bead represents a value of one. Some modern abacuses have one bead instead of two on the top section. The abacus is normally used for addition, subtraction, multiplication and division. It can also be used for fractions and square root, but this is not common. The abacus was often referred to as 'the first computer' as it was used as a mathematical model for early electronic computers. Although the abacus has now mostly been replaced by electronic calculators and computers, many traditionally styled shops such as herbal shops still use them. People world-wide learn to use the abacus as good mental training.

❀ Expressions using numbers

一心一意 — firmly make up one's mind
　　　　他一心一意要去美国念书。
　　　　He has set his mind on going to study in America.

三心两意 — cannot make up one's mind
　　　　他三心两意，不能做决定。
　　　　He is of two minds and unable to make a decision.

三三两两 — in groups of two or three
　　　　同学们三三两两的来了。
　　　　Fellow students have come in twos and threes.

不三不四 — dubious, shady
　　　　他常和不三不四的朋友在一起。
　　　　He often hangs around with friends of dubious character.

五花八门 — of a wide variety, all kinds of
　　　　那家店里卖的东西五花八门，什么都有。
　　　　That shop sells a great variety of goods; it has everything.

第四课 年轻人的世界
qīng

1 No big deal（没什么大不了）
liǎo

Listen and discuss -

1. What did Li Qiu do to Lanlan and why did she do that?
2. What happened to Lanlan? Why did it happen?
3. What was Li Qiu's response to Lanlan's decision?
4. How did Lanlan justify her decision?
5. What did Li Qiu think of Lanlan's mother? What was Lanlan's response to it?

（一）没什么大不了

嘿！！！

吓了我一跳！李秋。

对不起！你在想什么，发呆啊？

没想什么……唉！想看书，可是心情不好，看不下去。

怎么回事？为什么心情不好？

昨天我和他吹了。

你们吹了？为什么吹了？

我们觉得我们俩个性实在不合，所以就决定分手了。

别开玩笑了！他人帅，个子高，又到处出风头，是女孩子心目中的白马王子呢！

算了吧！其实他非常骄傲，都不把别人放在眼里。昨天我们吵了一架，就决定分手了。

个性不合，分手就分手了，别难过了。

我昨天晚上大哭了一场。不过现在想想，分手也没什么大不了，反正我妈妈本来就不赞成我交男朋友。

你妈妈不赞成你交男朋友？她要你一辈子不结婚啊？

别开玩笑了！她说中学生得好好儿学习，将来才能上好的大学。

资料箱

你看她在想什么？

你看她在想什么？

我看啊，她是在打瞌睡。

<ruby>打瞌睡<rt>kē shuì</rt></ruby>

打瞌睡

发<ruby>呆<rt>dāi</rt></ruby>

做白日<ruby>梦<rt>mèng</rt></ruby>

想她的白马<ruby>王<rt>wáng</rt></ruby>子

想她的男朋友

你希望你的男／女朋友长得怎么样？

我希望她长得很清秀。

我希望他长得很壮。

Well, save an arrow...

长得很<ruby>清秀<rt>qīng xiù</rt></ruby>

长得很迷人

又<ruby>漂亮<rt>piào liàng</rt></ruby>又<ruby>聪<rt>cōng</rt></ruby>明

长得很<ruby>壮<rt>zhuàng</rt></ruby>

长得很<ruby>帅<rt>shuài</rt></ruby>

个子很高

长得不错

他／她的个性怎么样？

她很善良。

人<ruby>缘<rt>yuán</rt></ruby>儿很好

很<ruby>善良<rt>shàn liáng</rt></ruby>

很<ruby>随<rt>suí</rt></ruby>和

很<ruby>骄傲<rt>jiāo ào</rt></ruby>

<ruby>爱<rt>ài</rt></ruby>出风头

爱开玩笑

脾气很坏

脾气很好

小世界

看不下去

王明美很喜欢看爱情小说。她常常一边看一

边哭，说故事很感人。昨

天她刚看完一本小说，我

就向她借来看。我的天！

实在很无聊，谈恋爱、做

白日梦、吵架、分手……。我实在看不下去。

吹就吹了

黄定交过很多女朋友。他每次交女朋友都

很快就吹了，可是他觉得吹就吹了，没什么大

不了的。他认为自己长得又高又帅，喜欢他的女

孩子很多。听说，他上个星期才和女朋友分手，

昨天又交了一个新的。我看啊，过几天他们就

会再吹了。

赞成

我妈妈很赞成我现在交女朋友。我的女朋友个性好，学习也认真。到我们家时，她常在厨房帮我妈妈的忙。她啊，是我妈妈心目中的好女孩。我妈妈非常喜欢她，还要我姐姐向她学习呢！

反对

我妈妈反对我现在交男朋友。她说上次姐姐交男朋友时常常很晚回家，学习也不用心，后来和男朋友分手时，又难过得书都念不下去，常常坐着发呆。妈妈不希望我和姐姐一样，所以非常反对我现在交男朋友。她要我在中学好好儿学习，等上了大学再交男朋友。

 聊天室

1. 你常发呆^{dāi}吗？为什么？
2. 你认为个性不合^{hé}的人可以在一起吗？为什么？
3. 你希望你的男／女朋友是什么样的人？
4. 你和谁吵^{chǎo}过架^{jià}？为什么吵架？
5. 你赞成中学生交男／女朋友吗？为什么？
6. 你父母亲赞成你现在交男／女朋友吗？为什么？

 男朋友

2 Just for fun（好玩而已）

Listen and discuss -

1. What was Li Qiu accusing Xiaoming of? What was the clue?
2. What did Xiaoming think about his own behavior?
3. What was Li Qiu's reaction to this behavior?
4. What advice did Li Qiu offer?
5. What did Li Qiu plead for and how did Xiaoming respond to it?

（二）好玩而已

🧑‍🦰 嘿！小明，你身上有烟味，是不是抽烟了？
_{hēi} _{shēn yān wèi} _{chōu}

👦 没有啊！

🧑‍🦰 说谎！我明明闻到烟味。快老实说来！
_{huǎng} _{wén}

👦 才抽一根而已啦！
_{gēn} _{la}

🧑‍🦰 学校不准我们抽烟，你是知道的。你哪儿来的香烟？
_{yān} _{xiāng}

👦 是一个十二年级的同学给我的。放心，没人看到。

🧑‍🦰 没人看到也不行。抽烟对身体有害，一旦上瘾就麻烦了。你得
_{chōu} _{tǐ hài} _{dàn yǐn má fán}
知道，"吸烟容易，戒烟难"。
_{xī róng yì jiè}

👦 我知道，我只是抽着好玩儿而已，不会上瘾的。

🧑‍🦰 算了吧！抽烟很容易上瘾，就跟吸毒一样。很多人刚开始吸
_{yǐn} _{xī dú} _{shǐ}
毒也只是吸着好玩儿，可是一旦上瘾就戒不掉了。你要知道，
_{dàn} _{jiè diào}
吸毒太多会死掉，抽烟太多会得肺癌。还有，你常在海边晒
_{sǐ} _{fèi ái} _{hǎi shài}
太阳，太阳晒太多会得皮肤癌……
_{yáng} _{pí fū ái}

👦 你有完没完？你知道吗？你最大的毛病就是爱小题大做！
_{wán} _{ài tí}

🧑‍🦰 随便你怎么说。反正抽不抽烟，一切在于你自己。
_{suí} _{yú}

资 料 箱

他为什么抽烟？
chōu yān

因为他觉得很酷。

好玩儿
他觉得很酷 kù
朋友都抽烟 chōu yān
朋友的怂恿 sǒng yǒng
他心情不好

做什么事很容易上瘾？ yǐn

抽烟很容易上瘾。

抽烟 chōu yān
吸毒 xī dú
看电视连续剧 lián xù jù
看足球赛 zú
玩电子游戏 xì
上网聊天
上网买东西
买名牌衣服

你最大的毛病是什么？

我常上课打瞌睡。

常让父母生气
常让老师生气
常上课打瞌睡 kē shuì
常花太多钱
老是忘了做作业
容易小题大做

小 世 界

说戒就戒

叔叔烟抽得很多，每天最少抽一包。

他说："戒烟很容易。我想抽就抽，说戒就戒。到现在，我抽烟已经抽了快十年了，戒烟也已经戒过十几次了。"

真的戒了

王平今年二十九岁。他抽烟抽了十几年了，每天最少抽一包。他知道抽烟对身体有害，也曾经戒过烟，可是都没成功。

今年王平交了一个女朋友。她不能吸二手烟。每次王平抽烟，她就咳嗽。王平就决定再戒烟。这次，王平真的把烟戒了。从四月开始戒烟到现在已经半年多了，王平都没再抽烟。大家都说："看起来，王平真的是很喜欢这个女朋友。"

谁说谎 (huǎng)

妈妈在浴室(yù)里看到了一包烟(yān)。她很生气，问(wèn)："这是谁的烟？"

姐姐说："那不是我的，也不是弟弟的。"

弟弟说："那不是我的，也不是哥哥的。"

哥哥说："那不是我的，我不知道是谁的。"

妈妈很不高兴(xing)，说他们三个人都在说谎(huǎng)。他们说，其实每一个人说的都有一半是真的。妈妈很快地就知道那包烟是谁的了。

小题大做

我女朋友比我妈妈还唠叨，又爱小题大做。我一玩电子游戏(xì)，她就唠叨说我玩上瘾(yǐn)了；我一抽烟(chōu yān)，她就告诉我将(jiāng)来会得肺癌(fèi ái)；我一晒太阳(shài yáng)，她就告诉我将来会得皮肤癌(pí fū ái)。我知道她是关心我，可是我实在不喜欢她这么小题大做。我告诉她，如果她再小题大做，将(jiāng)来就不是我的女朋友。

聊天室

1. 你对抽烟(chōu yān)有什么看法(fǎ)？
2. 你知道谁曾经戒(jiè)过烟？有没有成功？
3. 如果有人怂恿(sǒng yǒng)你吸毒(dú)，你怎么办(bàn)？
4. 如果你的朋友抽烟或吸毒，你怎么办？
5. 你最大的毛病是什么？
6. 你们班上谁最爱小题大做？

二手烟

两位先生，请进。

吸烟区(xī yān qū)还是非吸烟区(qū)？
非吸烟区
吸烟区
吸烟区。

1

2

这儿空气真差，到处都是烟味(wèi)。我们去非吸烟区(qū)吧。

不，我们还是坐这儿好。

为什么？你不是戒(jiè)烟了吗？

我是戒了。

3

4

那你为什么选(xuǎn)吸烟区(qū)呢？

因为医生只说不准我吸烟，他没说不准我吸二手烟(yā)呀！

5

6

3 **A little dilemma**（有点儿矛盾）

Listen and discuss -

1. What did Li Qiu and her friends do this afternoon? How did she feel afterward?
2. What trouble did she have when she got home?
3. What happened later in the evening?
4. How did Li Qiu feel about her mother's reaction?
5. What did Li Qiu think of her fashion sense?

（三）有点儿矛盾

今天上午我和班上的几个女孩子一起去逛街。临时有人提议去染头发，大家都赞成，我们就进了美容院。我把前面的头发染成紫色的，看起来还不错。后来又有人提议去穿肚脐洞。我本来不想去，可是同学们一直怂恿，也就跟着去了。穿了肚脐洞以后，我心里觉得怪怪的，不知道自己究竟喜欢还是不喜欢。

下午回到家里，妈妈一看到我的头发就开始唠叨，说年轻人不好好儿学习，爱作怪。到了晚上，妹妹把我戴肚脐环的事告诉了妈妈。妈妈更是大发脾气。

我觉得戴肚脐环也没什么大不了，妈妈实在太小题大做了。现在到处是新潮的年轻人，做各种奇怪的打扮。跟他们比起来，我已经是很保守了。妈妈平常还挺开通的，不知道为什么今天这么不开通。

老实说，戴不戴肚脐环，我心里也有点儿矛盾。戴肚脐环其实挺不方便的，说不定我过几天就把它拿下来。

资料箱

你的朋友会怂恿（sǒng yǒng）你做什么？

他们会怂恿我染头发。

买流行的服饰（shì）

染头发（rǎn）

穿肚脐洞（qí dòng）／戴肚脐环（dài）

穿耳洞（ěr）／戴耳环

文身（wén）

抽烟（chōu yān）

做奇怪的打扮（bàn）

年轻人常抱怨（bào yuàn）父母亲什么？

他们是老古板。

Try this, Dad!

是老古板（gǔ bǎn）

很不开通

太保守了（shǒu）

爱唠叨

爱小题大做

常发脾气

不关心我

不了解我（liǎo jiě）

他／她为什么心里觉得矛盾（máo dùn）？

因为她想减肥，又喜欢吃巧克力。

想减肥（jiǎn féi），又喜欢吃巧克力（qiǎo kè lì）

想存钱（cún），又喜欢买名牌衣服

想染头发（rǎn），又担心妈妈唠叨（dān）

想去旅行，又担心花钱

想打工，又担心忙不过来

小 世 界

怂恿
_{sǒng yǒng}

今天放学后，有同学提议去买烟来抽。
_{tí yì} _{yān} _{chōu}

我吓了一跳，告诉他们学校不准我们抽烟。
_{xià} _{tiào}

他们要我放心，就带我去学校后面，说没

人会看到，他们说："别小题大做，只是

抽着好玩而已啦！"我明明知道是不该抽
_{la}

的，可是他们一直怂恿，也就跟着抽了。老实说，
_{sǒng yǒng}

在回家的路上，我心里觉得怪怪的。我告诉自己，

下次一定不再跟他们去。

作怪

有人说，现在的年轻人很爱作怪，可是我

不这么认为。我有一个朋友，常常做奇怪的打
_{wéi}

扮，给人不好的印象。其实她人很好，对朋友
_{bàn}

很热心，做事也很认真。我一点都不觉得她是

爱作怪的人。

赞成

　　^{Chén}陈南说他的父母亲很开通。他们赞成他^{rǎn}染头发、穿^{ěr dòng}耳洞和穿^{qí}肚脐洞。他要^{wén}文身，他们也赞成。

不反对

　　黄爱容的父母亲都是很^{shǒu}保守的人。黄爱容的个性也很保守。她不穿太短的^{qún}裙子，不穿太瘦的衣服，不^{dài}戴^{qí}肚脐环，也不戴^{ěr}耳环。黄爱容说，她的父母亲很开通，她想做的事他们都不会反对。

^{xiāng máo dùn}自相矛盾

　　^{Wáng}王其说他父母亲的话常^{xiāng máo dùn}自相矛盾。他们常跟王其说，他们是很开通的父母，可是上次王其穿了两个^{ěr dòng}耳洞，他们就说他爱作怪，他^{rǎn}染头发时，他们也唠叨了半天。

 聊天室

1. 你染(rǎn)过头发吗？感觉怎么样？
2. 你的朋友会怂恿(sǒng yǒng)你做什么事？
3. 你觉得现在的年轻人很爱作怪吗？为什么？
4. 你觉得自己新潮(cháo)还是保守(shǒu)？为什么？
5. 你认为你父母亲开通吗(wéi)？为什么？
6. 什么事曾经让你心里觉得矛盾(máo dùn)？

自相矛盾

1. 快来买矛，我的矛(máo)是世界上最好的矛。

2. 你的矛有多好呢？

3. 可好呢！它可以刺穿任何(rèn hé)东西。
真好！真好！

4. 快来买盾，我的盾(dùn)是世界上最好的盾！

5. 你的盾有多好呢？

6. 可好呢！没有任何(rèn hé)东西可以刺穿它。
真好！真好！

7. 那么，如果拿(ná)你的矛来刺(cì)你的盾呢？
这，这⋯

例 句

1　**No big deal 没 什 么 大 不 了**

大不了^{liǎo}　**big deal** used colloquially, e.g. 没什么大不了 – no big deal; 有什么大不了
– what's the big deal.

我只是得了小感冒，没什么大不了^{liǎo}。

吸^{xī}烟^{yān}有什么大不了的？真是的！

下去　When 下去 is used following a verb, it indicates an action being continued.

v + 得下去　able to complete or carry on

v + 不下去　unable to complete or carry on

这本书很没意思，你看得下去吗？

我看不下去，这本书太没意思了。

他太累了，功课做不下去了。

出风头　**be in the spotlight; show off**

他球打得好，在球场上很出风头。

他人缘^{yuán}好，学习又好，在学校很出风头。

她太爱出风头了，很多人都不喜欢她。

心目^{mù}中　**in one's eyes**

弟弟是老师心目^{mù}中的好学生。

他长得帅^{shuài}，是女孩子心目中的白马王^{wáng}子。

在学生的心目中，他是一个好老师。

不把……放在眼^{yǎn}里　**paying no respect to...**

她很骄^{jiāo}傲^{ào}，都不把别人放在眼^{yǎn}里。

他上课一直讲^{jiǎng}话，都不把老师放在眼里。

就　(emphasizing word) When "就" is used between two repeated verbs, it indicates a suggestion of tolerating what has happened/will happen, or taking it with ease.

女朋友吹就吹了，不要难过了。

工作辞就辞了，没什么可惜的。

Use of 才

(1) **just; only**

学校才开学，我们就忙得不得了。

你今年才十四岁，还不可以开车。

(2) **(only...) then**　It indicates something with condition.

你得好好儿念书，将来才能上好的大学。

你要早点回家，你妈妈才不会担心。

(3) **as late as**　It indicates something has happened later than expected.

大家都早就来了，你怎么现在才来？

昨天的电影两点钟开始，可是他两点半才到。

2　**Just for fun**　好玩而已

明明　**clearly, obviously**　It is used to emphasize the authenticity of a statement. It is often followed by an outcome which is opposite to that statement.

天气预报明明说今天会是晴天，可是却下了大雨。

他明明说今天要来的，不知道为什么没来。

老实说来　**to speak out honestly**

你有没有男朋友？老实说来！

这包烟是不是你的？老实说来！

4

而已　**that's all**　It is often used together with "才", "只是" or words of similar meaning.

我只是开玩笑而已，你不要生气。

我只是上网聊天而已，我妈妈就唠叨了半天。

小题大做　**make a mountain out of a molehill**

他那个人就是喜欢小题大做。

我只迟到五分钟他就发脾气，真是小题大做。
　　　　　　zhōng

3　**A little dilemma**　有点儿矛盾

成　　v + 成　**become, into**　When used after a verb, 成 leads to a change.
　　　　　　　　　　　　　　rǎn
他今天把头发染成了黄色的。

老师昨天把我看成你了。

怪怪的　**odd, weird, strange**

他今天看起来怪怪的。

这道菜吃起来怪怪的。

今天天气怪怪的。

究竟 [jiūjìng] **actually, the very end**
　　jiū jìng
他究竟是去还是不去？

你究竟有没有女朋友？

告诉我，你究竟喜欢谁？

矛盾 [máodùn] **contradictory, having contradicting thoughts, in a dilemma**
　　　　　　　　　　　　　　　máo dùn
要不要跟男朋友分手，她的心里很矛盾。
　　　　　xiāng
他说话常常自相矛盾。

生 词

---

1 **No big deal** 没什么大不了

年轻人	niánqīng rén	*n.* young people　年轻 - young; 轻 - light
大不了	dàbùliǎo	*colloq.* big deal (没什么大不了 - no big deal)
吓一跳	xià yí tiào	*v.* startle (someone)　吓 - to scare, to frighten; 跳 - jump, to jump e.g. 吓我一跳 - (it) frightens me; 吓了一跳 - had a fright
发呆	fādāi	*v.* be lost in thought, stare blankly　发 - to send out; 呆 - stupid, dull
心情	xīnqíng	*n.* mood　心 - heart; 情 - feelings
吹	chuī	*colloq.* to break up, literally 'to blow'; *v.* to play (flute, recorder etc.); blow
不合	bùhé	*v.* incompatible　合 - to fit
决定	juédìng	*v.* decide　决 - to decide; 定 - certain, to set
分手	fēnshǒu	*v.* part company, break up　分 - *v.* to part; 手 - hand
帅	shuài	*adj.* handsome, good-looking
出风头	chūfēngtóu	*v.* be in the spotlight, be very popular, show off　风头 - public attention; 出 - to come out; 风 - wind; 头 - head
女孩子	nǚháizi	*n.* girl (boy - 男孩子)
心目中	xīnmùzhōng	*phr.* in one's eyes　心 - heart; 目 - eye; 中 - in, middle, center
白马王子	báimǎ-wángzǐ	*n.* prince charming　白马 - white horse; 王子 - prince; 王 - king
算了吧	suànleba	*colloq.* drop it, forget it
骄傲	jiāo'ào	*adj.* arrogant, conceited　骄 - arrogant; 傲 - arrogant
眼里	yǎnlǐ	*n.* inside one's eyes　眼 - eyes; 里 - inside
吵架	chǎojià	*v.* quarrel
难过	nánguò	*adj.* sad　难 - difficult; 过 - to pass
哭	kū	*v.* cry
反正	fǎnzhèng	*adv.* anyway, anyhow　反 - oppose, opposite; 正 - exact, straight
本来	běnlái	*adv.* originally, at first
赞成	zànchéng	*v.* approve of, agree with (反对 - oppose, be against) 赞 - to support; 成 - to become
男朋友	nánpéngyou	*n.* boyfriend　男 - male; 朋友 - friend
一辈子	yíbèizi	*n.* all one's life, a lifetime　辈 - generation
结婚	jiéhūn	*v.* marry, get married　结 - to tie; 婚 - marriage
将来	jiānglái	*n.* future　将 - to be going to; 来 - to come
白日梦	báirìmèng	*n.* daydream　白日 - daytime; 梦 - dream
女朋友	nǚpéngyou	*n.* girlfriend　女 - female; 朋友 - friend
清秀	qīngxiù	*adj.* delicate and pretty
迷人	mírén	*adj.* charming　迷 - to charm
壮	zhuàng	*adj.* strong, muscular
善良	shànliáng	*adj.* kind-hearted　善 - good; 良 - good

4

爱情	aìqíng	*n.* (romantic) love 爱 - love; 情 - feelings
小说	xiǎoshuō	*n.* novel
故事	gùshì	*n.* story, tale
感人	gǎnrén	*adj.* moving, touching 感 - to feel
完	wán	*v.* finish; *adj.* complete
恋爱	liàn'ài	*v.* love, be in love; 谈恋爱 - to fall in love
反对	fǎnduì	*v.* oppose, be against 反 - oppose, opposite; 对 - opposite, correct
念	niàn	*v.* study

2 Just for fun 好玩而已

而已	éryǐ	*part.* that's all, nothing more
身上	shēnshàng	*n.* on one's body 身 - body; 上 - on; to go to
味	wèi	*n.* smell, odor; taste, flavor
抽	chōu	*v.* smoke (cigarette, pipe); to take out, to draw
说谎	shuōhuǎng	*v.* lie 说 - to tell, to speak; 谎 - lie
明明	míngmíng	*adv.* clearly, obviously
闻	wén	*v.* smell
老实说来	lǎoshí shuō lái	*v.* speak out honestly 老实 - honestly, honest
根	gēn	*m.w.* [for cigarette]
香烟	xiāngyān	*n.* cigarette 香 - fragrant; 烟 - cigarette, smoke
身体	shēntǐ	*n.* body 身 - body; 体 - body
有害	yǒuhài	*adj.* harmful 害 - harm
一旦	yídàn	*adv.* once, in case, now that
上瘾	shàngyǐn	*v.* be addicted to 上 - to go to; 瘾 - addiction
容易	róngyì	*adj.* easy 容 - to contain, appearance; 易 - easy
戒烟	jièyān	*v.* quit smoking 戒 - to quit; 烟 - cigarette, smoke
难	nán	*adj.* difficult, hard
吸毒	xīdú	*v.* do drugs 吸 - to inhale; 毒 - poison, toxin
戒掉	jièdiào	*v.* quit 戒 - to quit; 掉 - [a particle]; away, out
死掉	sǐdiào	*v.* die
肺癌	fèi'ái	*n.* lung cancer 肺 - lung; 癌 - cancer
海边	hǎibiān	*n.* seashore, seaside, beach 海 - sea; 边 - side
晒	shài	*v.* shine upon
太阳	tàiyáng	*n.* sun
皮肤癌	pífū'ái	*n.* skin cancer 皮肤 - skin; 癌 - cancer
有完没完	yǒu wán méi wán	*colloq.* 'Do you have enough or not?' 完 - finish
毛病	máobìng	*n.* problem, shortcoming 毛 - body hair, fur, 10-cent unit; 病 - sick, illness
小题大做	xiǎotí-dàzuò	*idiom.* make a mountain out of a molehill
随	suí	*v.* follow, e.g. 随你怎么说 - say as you please
在于	zài yú	*v.* be determined by, depend on
生气	shēngqì	*v.* get angry, take offence

4

戒	jiè	*v.* quit, give up
最少	zuìshǎo	*adv.* at least
包	bāo	*m.w.* [for packages, bundles, etc.] pack; *v.* to wrap
成功	chénggōng	*v.* succeed, success　成 - to become; 功 - effort, skill
却	què	*adv.* but

3　A little dilemma　有点儿矛盾

矛盾	máodùn	*adj.* contradictory, having contradicting thoughts, be in a dilemma 矛 - spear; 盾 - shield
临时	línshí	*adv.* at the time (when something happens)
提议	tíyì	*v.* suggest　提 - to bring up; 议 - opinion, view
染	rǎn	*v.* dye
美容院	měiróngyuàn	*n.* beauty salon　美 - to beautify, beautiful; 容 - appearance; 院 - yard, certain building
成	chéng	*v.* become, turn into, e.g. 染成红色 - dye into red color
穿	chuān	*v.* pierce, penerate; wear, put on
肚脐	dùqí	*n.* navel, e.g. 肚脐洞 - navel piercing, 肚脐环 - navel ring
洞	dòng	*n.* hole
跟	gēn	*v.* follow or accompany; *conj.* and, with; *prep.* towards, with
怪怪的	guàiguàide	*adj.* odd, strange, weird　怪 - odd, strange
究竟	jiūjìng	*adv.* actually, the very end　究 - after all; 竟 - to complete, eventually
作怪	zuòguài	*v.* act mischievously, create mischief　作 - to do, to make; 怪 - odd, strange
戴	dài	*v.* wear (hat, glasses, ring, etc.)
环	huán	*n.* ring, hoop, e.g. 耳环 - earrings; 肚脐环 - navel ring
新潮	xīncháo	*n.* new trend; *adj.* trendy, fashionable　新 - new; 潮 - wave, tide
打扮	dǎbàn	*n.* style of dress; *v.* dress up　打 - to hit; 扮 - put on
保守	bǎoshǒu	*adj.* conservative　保 - to keep; 守 - to abide by, to observe
开通	kāitōng	*adj.* open-minded, liberal　开 - to open; 通 - through, to get through
说不定	shuōbúdìng	*adv.* perhaps, maybe　定 - to decide, certain
服饰	fúshì	*n.* dress and personal adornment
耳洞	ěrdòng	*n.* ear piercing　耳 - ear; 洞 - hole
耳环	ěrhuán	*n.* earrings　耳 - ear; 环 - ring, hoop
文身	wénshēn	*v & n.* tattoo　文 - to tattoo, lines; 身 - body
抱怨	bàoyuàn	*v.* complain　抱 - to hug, to embrace; 怨 - resentment, to blame
老古板	lǎogǔbǎn	*n.* old fogey　古 - ancient; 板 - board
了解	liǎojiě	*v.* understand; *n.* understanding
巧克力	qiǎokèlì	*n.* chocolate [transliteration]
自相矛盾	zìxiāng-máodùn	*idiom.* be self-contradictory　自 - self; 相 - mutual; 矛盾 - contradictory

学写字

Radical in color

情 **qíng** *feelings*	吹 **chuī** *to blow*	实 **shí** *fact, real*	决 **jué** *to decide*	笑 **xiào** *to smile, to laugh, smile*
处 **chù** *place*	出 **chū** *to go/come out*	孩 **hái** *child*	其 **qí** *that, such*	难 **nán** *difficult*
哭 **kū** *cry*	反 **fǎn** *oppose; opposite*	赞 **zàn** *to support*	借 **jiè** *to borrow*	身 **shēn** *body*
体 **tǐ** *body*	害 **hài** *harm*	容 **róng** *to contain; appearance*	易 **yì** *easy*	死 **sǐ** *to die; death*
完 **wán** *finish; complete*	爱 **ài** *to love; love*	题 **tí** *topic; question*	包 **bāo** *to wrap; bag*	逛 **guàng** *to stroll*
街 **jiē** *street*	美 **měi** *beautiful, to beautify*	怪 **guài** *odd, strange*	轻 **qīng** *light (in weight)*	奇 **qí** *unusual*

4

文化厅

🌸 Opium in China

Opium, 鸦片 yāpiàn, is not a native plant of China but was known by the Chinese in the very early years. According to literature, a miraculous doctor 华佗 huátuó in 东汉, the East Han Dynasty (25~220 AD), cut open and operated on his patients' abdomen using an anaesthetic drug. Although there is no concrete proof, some research suggests that the drug his patients drank might have contained opium.

Opium was officially recorded in the 7th century as one of the foreign tributes. It was rare and precious, and was used as medicine. In the 17th century, it appeared that traders were smuggling opium to China, and some privileged people started taking it for pleasure.

In the 19th century an influx of opium occurred. The West's demand for China's porcelain, tea and silk created a huge trade deficit for the West. To combat this deficit, Western traders such as the British East India Company shipped in large quantities of opium that was grown in India. With an ample supply, opium smoking spread from the privileged people to civilians. People lying in bed puffing the smoke became a social norm. Despite its efforts, the Chinese authority could not stop these illegal trades. In 1838, a determined officer, 林则徐 Lín Zéxú, confiscated over one thousand tons of opium from the Western traders and had it burnt. His act enraged the Westerners.

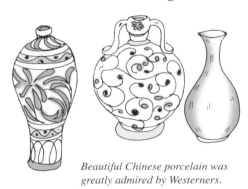

Beautiful Chinese porcelain was greatly admired by Westerners.

Wars broke out which the Chinese called the Opium Wars, 鸦片战争 Yāpiàn Zhànzhēng. China was defeated, and signed treaties that included legalizing the opium trade and losing sovereignty over its ports.

Opium smoking worsened for a few more decades and carried on through numerous civil wars and the two World Wars. After painstaking efforts from all parties, the Chinese were finally rid of opium addiction in the mid-20th century.

Opium use during the Qing dynasty was not an uncommon sight.

✽ Golden lotus 三寸金莲

People admire beauty. The concept of beauty varies between different cultures and at different periods of time. In China around 清朝, the Qing Dynasty, women having small, bound feet was so fashionable that women were only considered to look graceful with tiny, bound feet, and a family's status also required presenting their daughters in this fashion.

The origin of bound feet started much earlier than 清朝. In the 10th century, Emperor 李后主 Lǐ Hòuzhǔ adored the graceful dance and the beautiful small feet of one of his court dancers. He built a dance stadium of golden lotus for her. To please the emperor, the dancer bound her feet in silk cloth and danced on the lotus. Small, bound feet thereafter became the pursuit of female entertainers, and eventually they also won admirers among high ranking people. Many literary works profusely described how these plump and tiny feet were caressed. Three-inch golden lotus, 三寸金莲 sān cùn jīn lián, was the best known description for them. Foot-binding became common in 清朝 among the Han people when the country was under the reign of the minority people, the Manchurian. The practice represented the Han people's pride, and was treated as a symbol of their family status. Parents bound their daughters' feet with layers of cloth to hinder growth, for the prospects of maintaining their family status and of their daughters marrying into respected families. Throughout their lives those women with bound feet were so confined that support was needed when they ventured out.

To eliminate this practice, a social unity was critical. Advocators had to form clubs so as to ensure that their daughters' future marriages would not be disadvantaged. Small, bound feet finally became history in the early 20th century. As a reminder, people sometimes describe a long and boring speech as 女人的缠脚布 nǚrén de chánjiǎobù, women's foot-binding cloth, 又臭又长 yòu chòu yòu cháng, long and smelly.

(Left and above) Small bound feet were considered to look graceful and were highly regarded as a symbol of family status despite the physical pain and side effects.

4

Suntan or no suntan

With their lighter complexions many Westerners risk their health in exposing themselves to the sun for a good-looking suntan. To the Chinese and many other Asians, having dark, tanned skin represents a harsh life of physically labor-intensive work in the sun. It is considered beautiful to have a light complexion. Women, young and old, do their best to stay out of the sun. Colorful umbrellas parading the streets is a scene on hot, sunny days.

Street scene of people with umbrellas, walking or even riding bicycles

Useful idioms

自相矛盾 – self-contradictory, inconsistent

他说的和做的常常自相矛盾。

What he does is often opposite to what he says.

你说话常常前后自相矛盾。

You always say things that are inconsistent.

哭笑不得 – not know whether to laugh or cry; feeling something annoying yet funny

弟弟说家里的狗吃了他的作业，实在让妈妈哭笑不得。

Little brother said our dog ate his homework and mom just doesn't know whether to laugh or cry.

平易近人 – *adj.* amiable and approachable

我们的校长很平易近人。

Our principal is amiable and approachable.

左右为难 – *adj.* be in a dilemma; not know which side to turn to

我不想去，可是老师要我去。我实在左右为难。

I don't feel like going but our teacher asked me to go. I am really in a dilemma.

少见多怪 – to wonder much because one has seen little; to make a fuss about nothing

这有什么大不了的？真是少见多怪！

What's the big deal about this? You are really making a fuss about it.

这实在没什么，别少见多怪了。

This is really nothing so don't be ignorant and overreact.

见怪不怪 – become inured to weird things; viewing weird things as nothing unusual

他就是喜欢做奇怪的打扮，我们已经见怪不怪了。

She always likes to dress weirdly and we have become used to it.

这种事我们看太多了，已经见怪不怪了。

We have seen too many of these things and no longer consider them strange.

Appendix 1

WORDS AND EXPRESSIONS
Chinese-English

(Words and expressions that did not appear in the main text are displayed in purple.)

	Simplified	Pinyin	English	Traditional	Lesson
A	爱情	àiqíng	*n.* (romantic) love	愛情	4-1
B	把	bǎ	*prep.* indicative word, see p. 19	把	1-1
	白马王子	báimǎ-wángzǐ	*n.* prince charming	白馬王子	4-1
	白日梦	báirìmèng	*n.* daydream	白日夢	4-1
	摆	bǎi	*v.* set up, arrange, place	擺	1-2
	班会	bānhuì	*n.* class meeting	班會	1-1
	班上	bānshàng	in the class	班上	1-2
	班长	bānzhǎng	*n.* class leader	班長	1-1
	班主任	bānzhǔrèn	*n.* form teacher, homeroom teacher	班主任	1-1
	半死	bànsǐ	*adj.* half dead	半死	3-1
	帮忙	bāngmáng	*adj.* helpful; *v.* help	幫忙	1-1
	棒	bàng	*adj.* [oral] excellent, good	棒	2-3
	傍晚	bàngwǎn	*n.* dusk, early evening	傍晚	2-3
	包	bāo	*v.* to wrap; *m.w.* [for packages, bundles, etc.] pack	包	2-2, 4-2
	饱	bǎo	*adj.* be full	飽	2-1
	保护	bǎohù	*v.* protect; *n.* protection	保護	2-3
	保龄球	bǎolíngqiú	*n.* bowling (tenpin) [transliteration]	保齡球	3-1
	保守	bǎoshǒu	*adj.* conservative	保守	4-3
	抱怨	bàoyuàn	*v.* complain	抱怨	4-3
	报纸	bàozhǐ	*n.* newspaper	報紙	2-2
	北美洲	Běi Měizhōu	*n.* North America	北美洲	2-3
	本来	běnlái	*adv.* originally, at first	本來	4-1
	表演	biǎoyǎn	*v.* to perform an act	表演	1-2
	别人	biérén	*n.* other people	別人	3-3
	不但	búdàn	*conj.* not only	不但	3-2
	不得了	bùdéliǎo	*adv.* extremely, exceedingly, see p. 22	不得了	1-2
	不合	bùhé	*v.* incompatible	不合	4-1
	不同	bùtóng	*adj.* different	不同	2-1
	不准	bùzhǔn	*v.* not allow, forbid	不准	1-3
C	才	cái	*adv.* just, only just	才	1-1
	餐馆	cānguǎn	*n.* restaurant	餐館	3-2
	藏	cáng	*v.* hide	藏	3-2
	曾经	céngjīng	*adv.* once, formerly, ever	曾經	3-2
	唱片行	chàngpiànháng	*n.* music store	唱片行	3-1
	吵	chǎo	*adj.* noisy; *v.* disturb, quarrel	吵	3-3
	吵架	chǎojià	*v.* quarrel	吵架	4-1
	成	chéng	*v.* become, turn into	成	4-3
	成功	chénggōng	*v.* succeed, success	成功	4-2

Simplified	Pinyin	English	Traditional	Lesson
成为	chéngwéi	*v.* become	成為	1-1
抽	chōu	*v.* smoke (cigarette, pipe); to take out, to draw	抽	4-2
出风头	chūfēngtóu	*v.* be in the spotlight, be very popular; show off	出風頭	4-1
除了……以外	chúle...yǐwài	*prep.* 1. besides, in addition to; 2. except	除了……以外	1-2
穿	chuān	*v.* pierce, penerate; wear, put on	穿	4-3
传真	chuánzhēn	*n.* facsimile	傳真	1-3
闯	chuǎng	*v.* rush; force one's way in or out	闖	2-1
吹	chuī	*colloq.* break up (with girlfriend or boyfriend)	吹	4-1
春假	chūnjià	*n.* spring holiday	春假	2-3
辞	cí	*v.* quit, resign, sack	辭	3-2
刺	cì	*v.* poke	刺	4-3
存	cún	*v.* save, deposit	存	3-3

D 打瞌睡	dǎ kēshuì	*v.* doze off	打瞌睡	2-3
打招呼	dǎ zhāohu	*v.* greet somebody	打招呼	2-1
打扮	dǎbàn	*n.* style of dress; *v.* dress up	打扮	4-3
打工	dǎgōng	*v.* have a part-time job	打工	3-1
打扰	dǎrǎo	*v.* disturb	打擾	1-2
大不了	dàbùliǎo	*colloq.* big deal	大不了	4-1
大熊猫	dàxióngmāo	*n.* giant panda	大熊貓	2-3
戴	dài	*v.* wear (hat, glasses, ring, etc.)	戴	4-3
袋鼠	dàishǔ	*n.* kangaroo	袋鼠	2-3
但是	dànshì	*conj.* but, yet, still, nevertheless	但是	1-2
当	dāng	*v.* be, work as, serve as, e.g. 当班长，当老师	當	1-1
	dàng	*n.* treat as; regard as, e.g. 当自己人		2-3
当时	dāngshí	*adv.* at that time, then	當時	3-1
捣蛋	dǎodàn	*v.* make trouble	搗蛋	2-3
到处	dàochù	*adv.* everywhere	到處	3-2
道歉	dàoqiàn	*v.* apologize	道歉	1-3
等	děng	*pron.* and so on, and so forth; *v.* wait	等	1-2
低	dī	*adj.* low	低	3-2
地方	dìfāng	*adj.* local; *n.* place, location	地方	3-1
店	diàn	*n.* shop, store	店	3-1
店员	diànyuán	*n.* clerk, salesperson	店員	3-1
电影院	diànyǐngyuàn	*n.* cinema	電影院	1-1
电子	diànzǐ	*n.* electronic, e-	電子	1-3
电子邮件	diànzǐ yóujiàn	*n.* e-mail	電子郵件	1-3
电子游戏	diànzǐ yóuxì	*n.* computer game, video game	電子遊戲	1-3
电子邮址	diànzǐ yóuzhǐ	*n.* e-mail address	電子郵址	1-3
顶	dǐng	*m.w.* [for something with a top]	頂	3-2
丢	diū	*v.* throw; lose	丟	2-2
丢人	diūrén	*colloq.* embarrassing; *v.* lose face	丟人	2-2
洞	dòng	*n.* hole	洞	4-3
动物园	dòngwùyuán	*n.* zoo	動物園	2-3
动心	dòngxīn	*adj.* heart set on something, be tempted	動心	3-3
堵车	dǔchē	*v.* have a traffic jam	堵車	2-1
肚脐	dùqí	*n.* navel	肚臍	4-3
肚脐洞	dùqídòng	*n.* navel piercing	肚臍洞	4-3
肚脐环	dùqíhuán	*n.* navel ring	肚臍環	4-3
队	duì	*n.* team, group	隊	1-2

Simplified	Pinyin	English	Traditional	Lesson
对联	duìlián	*n.* a Chinese couplet written on scrolls etc.	對聯	2-3
盾	dùn	*n.* shield	盾	4-3
多半	duōbàn	*adv.* mostly	多半	2-1

E

Simplified	Pinyin	English	Traditional	Lesson
而且	érqiě	*conj.* also, moreover, in addition	而且	3-2
而已	éryǐ	*part.* that's all, nothing more	而已	4-2
耳洞	ěrdòng	*n.* ear piercing	耳洞	4-3
耳环	ěrhuán	*n.* earrings	耳環	4-3
二手烟	èrshǒuyān	*n.* passive smoking	二手煙	3-2

F

Simplified	Pinyin	English	Traditional	Lesson
发呆	fādāi	*v.* be lost in thought, stare blankly	發呆	4-1
发问	fāwèn	*v.* ask or raise a question	發問	2-3
翻	fān	*v.* turn over	翻	1-1
反对	fǎnduì	*v.* oppose, be against	反對	4-1
反正	fǎnzhèng	*adv.* anyway, anyhow	反正	4-1
方便	fāngbiàn	*adj.* convenient	方便	1-3
放假	fàngjià	*v.* have a holiday or vacation	放假	1-1
放心	fàngxīn	*v.* stop worrying, be at ease	放心	1-1
非	fēi	*adj.* non-, un-, etc.	非	4-2
非吸烟区	fēi xīyān qū	*n.* non-smoking area	非吸煙區	4-2
非洲	Fēizhōu	*n.* Africa	非洲	2-3
肺癌	fèi'ái	*n.* lung cancer	肺癌	4-2
分手	fēnshǒu	*v.* break up, part company	分手	4-1
份	fèn	*m.w.* [for work, newspaper, magazine etc.]	份	3-1
封	fēng	*m.w.* [for letter]	封	1-3
风景	fēngjǐng	*n.* scenery	風景	2-1
风土人情	fēngtǔrénqíng	local conditions and customs	風土人情	2-1
服饰	fúshì	*n.* dress and personal adornment	服飾	4-3
服饰店	fúshìdiàn	*n.* fashion shop	服飾店	3-3
服务员	fúwùyuán	*n.* attendant	服務員	3-1
副	fù	*m.w.* pair	副	2-3
付	fù	*v.* pay	付	3-2
附近	fùjìn	*adj.* nearby, in the vicinity	附近	2-2
父母亲	fùmǔqīn	*n.* parents	父母親	2-2
父亲	fùqīn	*n.* father	父親	2-2

G

Simplified	Pinyin	English	Traditional	Lesson
改	gǎi	*v.* change	改	1-3
赶	gǎn	*v.* catch up with; hurry, rush	趕	3-3
感觉	gǎnjué	*n.* feeling; *v.* feel	感覺	2-2
感人	gǎnrén	*adj.* moving, touching	感人	4-1
刚好	gānghǎo	*adv.* just, so happen that	剛好	3-1
高尔夫球	gāo'ěrfūqiú	*n.* golf	高爾夫球	1-2
高兴	gāoxìng	*adj.* happy	高興	1-2
告诉	gàosù	*v.* tell, let know	告訴	1-1
各地	gèdì	*adv.* every region	各地	2-1
各种	gèzhǒng	*n.* various kinds	各種	2-1
跟	gēn	*prep.* towards or with; *conj.* and;	跟	3-1
		v. follow or accompany		4-3
根	gēn	*m.w.* [for cigarette]	根	4-2
功能	gōngnéng	*n.* function	功能	1-3

Simplified	Pinyin	English	Traditional	Lesson
公园	gōngyuán	*n.* park	公園	2-2
工资	gōngzī	*n.* salary, wage	工資	3-1
工作	gōngzuò	*n.* work, job; *v.* to work	工作	3-2
古迹	gǔjì	*n.* historic site	古蹟	2-1
顾客	gùkè	*n.* customer, client	顧客	3-2
故事	gùshì	*n.* story, tale	故事	4-1
怪怪的	guàiguàide	*adj.* odd, strange, weird	怪怪的	4-3
关心	guānxīn	*v.* care about	關心	1-1
罐子	guànzi	*n.* tin, can, jar	罐子	2-2
光盘	guāngpán	*n.* CD, DVD or VCD, called 光碟 guāngdié in Taiwan	光盤	1-3
逛街	guàngjiē	*v.* go window-shopping, stroll around the street	逛街	1-1
贵	guì	a respectful form of "your", used in formal occasions	貴	1-1
国际象棋	guójì xiàngqí	*n.* chess	國際象棋	1-2
过来	guòlái	(1) *v.* come over; (2) used after a verb, preceded by "得" to indicate possibility, see p. 20	過來	1-1
过瘾	guòyǐn	*adj.* enjoy oneself to the full	過癮	1-2

H

Simplified	Pinyin	English	Traditional	Lesson
海边	hǎibiān	*n.* seashore, seaside, beach	海邊	1-1, 4-2
好用	hǎoyòng	*adj.* be convenient to use	好用	1-3
好客	hàokè	*adj.* be hospitable	好客	2-1
合唱团	héchàngtuán	*n.* choir	合唱團	1-2
河马	hémǎ	*n.* hippopotamus	河馬	2-3
和尚	héshàng	*n.* Buddhist monk	和尚	2-3
花	huā	*v.* spend, e.g. 花钱 - to spend money; *n.* flower	花	3-1
划船	huáchuán	*n.* rowing; *v.* row a boat	划船	1-2
环	huán	*n.* ring, hoop; *v.* surround	環	2-2, 4-3
环保	huánbǎo	*n.* environmental protection	環保	2-2
环境	huánjìng	*n.* environment	環境	3-2
谎	huǎng	*n.* lie	謊	4-2
回报	huíbào	*n.* return, reward	回報	3-1
回收	huíshōu	*v.* recycle	回收	2-2
回头	huítóu	*v.* turn one's head, turn around	回收	2-3
活动	huódòng	*n.* activity	活動	1-1
火锅	huǒguō	*n.* hot pot	火鍋	2-2
或	huò	*conj.* or, either or	或	3-1

J

Simplified	Pinyin	English	Traditional	Lesson
几乎	jīhū	*adv.* almost	幾乎	2-3
机会	jīhuì	*n.* chance, opportunity	機會	2-1
极	jí	*adv.* extremely, exceedingly	極	3-2
记得	jìde	*v.* remember	記得	2-2
佳	jiā	*adj.* good, fine	佳	1-1
家教	jiājiào	*n.* private tutor	家教	3-1
家事	jiāshì	*n.* housework	家事	3-3
加入	jiārù	*v.* join in	加入	1-2
加温	jiāwēn	*v.* heat	加溫	2-3
价钱	jiàqián	*n.* price	價錢	3-3
见面	jiànmiàn	*v.* to meet, see	見面	1-1
将来	jiānglái	*n.* future	將來	4-1
讲话	jiǎnghuà	*v.* talk, speak	講話	2-3
交	jiāo	*v.* to cross, to interact; to hand in	交	1-1
交换	jiāohuàn	*v.* exchange, swap	交換	2-1

Simplified	Pinyin	English	Traditional	Lesson
交通	jiāotōng	*n.* traffic	交通	2-1
交响乐	jiāoxiǎngyuè	*n.* symphony	交響樂	1-2
骄傲	jiāo'ào	*adj.* arrogant, conceited	驕傲	4-1
结婚	jiéhūn	*v.* marry, get married	結婚	4-1
戒	jiè	*v.* quit, give up	戒	4-2
戒掉	jièdiào	*v.* quit	戒掉	4-2
戒烟	jièyān	*v.* quit smoking	戒煙	4-2
进	jìn	*v.* to enter	進	3-3
经验	jīngyàn	*n.* experience	經驗	3-1
究竟	jiūjìng	*adv.* actually, the very end	究竟	4-3
旧	jiù	*adj.* used, worn, old	舊	3-2
拘束	jūshù	*v.* restrict, restrain	拘束	2-2
决定	juédìng	*v.* decide	決定	4-1
K 咖啡	kāfēi	*n.* coffee	咖啡	2-1, 2-2
开始	kāishǐ	*v.* begin, start	開始	1-1
开通	kāitōng	*adj.* open-minded, liberal	開通	4-3
开心	kāixīn	*v.* feel happy, rejoice	開心	1-1
开学	kāixué	*v.* school starts	開學	1-1
看法	kànfǎ	*n.* viewpoint, opinion	看法	4-2
考拉	kǎolā	*n.* koala [transliteration]	考拉	2-3
烤肉	kǎoròu	*v. & n.* barbecue	烤肉	2-2
可乐	kělè	*n.* cola [transliteration]	可樂	2-2
可惜	kěxī	it's a pity, too bad	可惜	3-2
课外	kèwài	*adj.* extracurricular	課外	1-2
空	kōng	*adj.* empty	空	2-2
空气	kōngqì	*n.* air	空氣	2-1
空手道	kōngshǒudào	*n.* karate	空手道	1-2
哭	kū	*v.* cry	哭	4-1
酷	kù	*slang* cool [transliteration]; cruel, extreme	酷	3-3
快餐	kuàicān	*n.* fast food	快餐	3-1
快点儿	kuàidiǎnr	*v.* hurry up	快點兒	1-2
宽敞	kuānchang	*adj.* spacious, roomy	寬敞	2-3
L 垃圾	lājī, lèsè	*n.* rubbish, garbage	垃圾	2-2
懒洋洋	lǎnyángyáng	*adj.* sluggish, listless	懶洋洋	2-3
浪费	làngfèi	*v.* waste; *adj.* wasteful	浪費	1-3
唠叨	láodao	*v.* nag	嘮叨	3-3
老板	lǎobǎn	*n.* boss	老闆	3-2
老古板	lǎogǔbǎn	*n.* old fogey	老古板	4-3
老实说来	lǎoshí shuō lái	*v.* speak out honestly	老實說來	4-2
老是	lǎoshì	*adv.* always, all the time	老是	3-1
垒球	lěiqiú	*n.* softball	壘球	1-2
累	lèi	*adj.* tired, fatigued	累	3-1
离开	líkāi	*v.* leave	離開	4-1
例句	lìjù	*n.* example sentence	例句	1-1
利用	lìyòng	*v.* use, make use of	利用	1-3
联系	liánxì	*v.* contact, get in touch with	聯繫	1-3
练	liàn	*v.* practise	練	1-2
练习	liànxí	*n.* exercise, practice	練習	1-2
恋爱	liàn'ài	*v.* love, be in love	戀愛	4-1

Simplified	Pinyin	English	Traditional	Lesson
辆	liàng	*m.w.* [for car, bus, bicycle, etc.]	輛	3-3
聊天	liáotiān	*v.* chat	聊天	1-3
聊天室	liáotiān shì	*n.* chat room	聊天室	1-1, 1-3
了解	liǎojiě	*v.* understand; *n.* understanding	了解	4-3
料子	liàozi	*n.* material (fabric)	料子	3-3
临时	línshí	*adv.* at the time (when something happens)	臨時	4-3
零花	línghuā	*v.* spend pocket money	零花	3-3
零花钱	línghuāqián	*n.* pocket money	零花錢	3-1
留	liú	*v.* leave behind; remain, stay; reserve, save	留	2-3
流行	liúxíng	*adj.* popular, in fashion	流行	3-1
路过	lùguò	*v.* pass by	路過	2-1
旅行团	lǔxíngtuán	*n.* tourist group	旅行團	2-1
乱	luàn	*adj.* in disorder, messy	亂	3-2
M 麻烦	máfan	*adj.* troublesome, inconvenient	麻煩	2-2
骂	mà	*v.* scold, condemn	罵	1-3
慢	màn	*adv & adj.* slow	慢	1-3
矛	máo	*n.* spear	矛	4-3
矛盾	máodùn	*adj.* contradictory, having contradicting thoughts, be in a dilemma	矛盾	4-3
毛病	máobìng	*n.* problem, shortcoming	毛病	4-2
帽子	màozi	*n.* hat	帽子	3-2
美容院	měiróngyuàn	*n.* beauty salon	美容院	4-3
每天	měitiān	*n.* everyday	每天	2-3
迷人	mírén	*adj.* charming	迷人	4-1
面包	miànbāo	*n.* bread	麵包	2-2
明明	míngmíng	*adv.* clearly, obviously	明明	4-2
名牌	míngpái	*n.* famous brand	名牌	3-3
名胜	míngshèng	*n.* well-known scenic spot	名勝	2-1
母亲	mǔqīn	*n.* mother	母親	2-2
木	mù	*n.* tree, wood	木	1-1
N 难	nán	*adj.* difficult, hard	難	4-2
难过	nánguò	*adj.* sad	難過	4-1
男朋友	nánpéngyou	*n.* boyfriend	男朋友	4-1
年轻人	niánqīng rén	*n.* young people	年輕人	4-1
念	niàn	*v.* study	念	4-1
牛排	niúpái	*n.* steak	牛排	2-2
女孩子	nǔháizi	*n.* girl	女孩子	4-1
女朋友	nǔpéngyou	*n.* girlfriend	女朋友	4-1
P 拍照	pāizhào	*v.* take a picture	拍照	1-3
排球	páiqiú	*n.* volleyball	排球	1-2
盘子	pánzi	*n.* plate	盤子	2-2
泡	pào	*v.* brew (tea or coffee), soak	泡	2-3
皮肤癌	pífū'ái	*n.* skin cancer	皮膚癌	4-2
啤酒	píjiǔ	*n.* beer	啤酒	2-2
脾气	píqi	*n.* temper	脾氣	3-2
瓶子	píngzi	*n.* bottle, vase	瓶子	2-2
普通话	pǔtōnghuà	*n.* Mandarin, literally common speech	普通話	2-1

	Simplified	Pinyin	English	Traditional	Lesson
Q	妻子	qīzi	*n.* wife (formal term)	妻子	2-3
	其实	qíshí	*adv.* actually, in fact	其實	1-3
	奇异鸟	qíyìniǎo	*n.* kiwi bird	奇異鳥	2-3
	气候	qìhòu	*n.* climate	氣候	2-1
	巧克力	qiǎokèlì	*n.* chocolate	巧克力	4-3
	轻松	qīngsōng	*adj.* relaxed	輕鬆	3-2
	清秀	qīngxiù	*adj.* delicate and pretty	清秀	4-1
	却	què	*adv.* but	卻	4-2
R	然后	ránhòu	*adv.* afterwards, then	然後	2-3
	染	rǎn	*v.* dye	染	4-3
	让	ràng	*v.* give way; let, allow	讓	2-1
	热心	rèxīn	*adj.* enthusiastic	熱心	1-1
	人选	rénxuǎn	*n.* candidate	人選	1-1
	人缘儿	rényuánr	*n.* relations with people; popularity	人緣兒	1-1
	任何	rènhé	*adj.* any, whatever	任何	4-3
	认为	rènwéi	*v.* think, consider	認為	1-1
	容易	róngyì	*adj.* easy	容易	4-2
	肉串	ròuchuàn	*n.* kebab	肉串	2-2
	入乡随俗	rù xiāng suí sú	*idiom* when in Rome, do as the Romans do	入鄉隨俗	2-1
	软体	ruǎntǐ	*n.* software	軟體	1-3
S	沙拉	shālā	*n.* salad [transliteration]	沙拉	2-2
	晒	shài	*v.* shine upon	曬	4-2
	善良	shànliáng	*adj.* kind-hearted	善良	4-1
	上网	shàng wǎng	*v.* get on the internet	上網	1-3
	上衣	shàngyī	*n.* upper garment	上衣	3-3
	上瘾	shàngyǐn	*v.* be addicted to	上癮	4-2
	社	shè	*n.* club or society of special interest or purpose	社	1-2
	设计	shèjì	*v. & n.* design	設計	1-3
	深	shēn	*adj.* deep; dark	深	2-1
	身上	shēnshàng	*n.* on one's body	身上	4-2
	身体	shēntǐ	*n.* body	身體	4-2
	声	shēng	*n.* sound; voice	聲	3-3
	生词	shēngcí	*n.* new word	生詞	1-1
	生气	shēngqì	*v.* get angry, take offence	生氣	4-2
	十分	shífēn	*adv.* very, fully, extremely	十分	2-1
	实在	shízài	*adv.* really	實在	2-2
	试穿	shìchuān	*v.* try on (clothes/shoes)	試穿	3-3
	世界	shìjiè	*n.* world	世界	1-1, 2-1
	式样	shìyàng	*n.* style	式樣	3-3
	收	shōu	*v.* to collect, to receive	收	1-1
	收据	shōujù	*n.* receipt	收據	3-2
	收拾	shōushi	*v.* tidy up, put in order	收拾	2-2
	受不了	shòu bù liǎo	*colloq.* cannot endure; unbearable; intolerable	受不了	3-2
	输	shū	*v.* lose; be beaten	輸	1-2
	帅	shuài	*adj.* handsome, good-looking	帥	4-1
	双	shuāng	*m.w.* [for shoes, socks etc.] pair	雙	1-1
	水平	shuǐpíng	*n.* standard, level	水平	3-2
	说不定	shuōbúdìng	*adv.* perhaps, maybe	說不定	4-3

Simplified	Pinyin	English	Traditional	Lesson
说谎	shuōhuǎng	*v.* lie	說謊	4-2
死掉	sǐdiào	*v.* die	死掉	4-2
死机	sǐjī	*v.* breakdown (computer)	死機	3-2
寺庙	sìmiào	*n.* temple	寺廟	2-3
怂恿	sǒngyǒng	*v.* urge, egg on	慫恿	3-3
宋代	Sòng Dài	*n.* Song Dynasty (960 - 1279 AD)	宋代	2-3
送报员	sòngbàoyuán	*n.* newsboy	送報員	3-1
苏东坡	Sū Dōngpō	*n.* a famous man of letters in Song dynasty	蘇東坡	2-3
塑料袋	sùliàodài	*n.* plastic bag	塑料袋	2-2
算了吧	suànleba	*colloq.* drop it, forget it	算了吧	4-1
虽然	suīrán	*conj.* although	雖然	1-2
随	suí	*v.* follow	隨	4-2
随你怎么说	suí nǐ zěnme shuō	*colloq.* say as you please	隨你怎麼說	4-2
随便	suíbiàn	*adj.* easy going, not fussy	隨便	2-1
随身听	suíshēntīng	*n.* portable listening device, e.g. walkman, ipod, MP3	隨身聽	3-3

T 态度	tàidù	*n.* attitude	態度	3-2
太阳	tàiyáng	*n.* sun	太陽	4-2
太阳能	tàiyángnéng	*n.* solar energy	太陽能	2-3
摊位	tānwèi	*n.* stand, stall	攤位	1-2
谈得来	tán de lái	*v.* get along well, usually have a good time chatting	談得來	1-1
特有	tèyǒu	*adj.* peculiar	特有	2-3
提议	tíyì	*v.* suggest	提議	4-3
体操	tǐcāo	*n.* gymnastics	體操	1-2
体验	tǐyàn	*v.* experience	體驗	2-1
听说	tīngshuō	*v.* be told, hear of, it is said	聽說	1-1
通常	tōngcháng	*adv.* usually	通常	1-3
桶	tǒng	*n.* bin, bucket, barrel	桶	2-2
秃鹰	tūyīng	*n.* bald eagle	禿鷹	2-3
吐	tù	*v.* to vomit, throw up	吐	1-1
团	tuán	*n.* group, organization	團	1-2
退	tuì	*v.* return (things)	退	3-2

W 完	wán	*v.* finish; *adj.* complete	完	4-1
网页	wǎngyè	*n.* web page	網頁	1-3
网友	wǎngyǒu	*n.* internet friend	網友	1-3
网址	wǎngzhǐ	*n.* website	網址	1-3
位	wèi	*m.w.* [for people - polite form]	位	1-1
喂	wèi	*v.* feed; *int.* hello	餵	2-3
味	wèi	*n.* smell, odor; taste, flavor	味	4-2
温水游泳池	wēnshuǐ yóuyǒngchí	*n.* heated pool	溫水游泳池	2-3
闻	wén	*v.* smell	聞	4-2
文身	wénshēn	*v & n.* tattoo	紋身	4-3
文学家	wénxuéjiā	*n.* writer, person of letters	文學家	2-3
我的天	wǒ de tiān	*colloq.* Oh my God!	我的天	3-2
无所不谈	wú suǒ bù tán	*idiom.* chat freely	無所不談	2-1
舞会	wǔhuì	*n.* dance party	舞會	1-2

X 吸毒	xīdú	*v.* do drugs	吸毒	4-2
吸烟	xīyān	*v.* smoke	吸煙	3-2
西方	xīfāng	*n.* the West	西方	2-1

Simplified	Pinyin	English	Traditional	Lesson
希望	xīwàng	*v.* hope	希望	2-2
习惯	xíguàn	*v.* get used to	習慣	2-1
洗澡	xǐzǎo	*v.* take a bath	洗澡	2-3
吓一跳	xià yí tiào	*v.* startle (someone)	嚇一跳	4-1
下载	xiàzǎi	*v.* download	下載	1-3
箱	xiāng	*n.* box	箱	1-1
香肠	xiāngcháng	*n.* sausage	香腸	2-2
香烟	xiāngyān	*n.* cigarette	香煙	4-2
项目	xiàngmù	*n.* item	項目	1-2
小吃	xiǎochī	*n.* snack	小吃	2-1
小孩	xiǎohái	*n.* children	小孩	2-2
小说	xiǎoshuō	*n.* novel	小說	4-1
小题大做	xiǎotí-dàzuò	*idiom.* make a mountain out of a molehill	小題大做	4-2
小心	xiǎoxīn	*v.* be careful, take care	小心	2-3
鞋	xié	*n.* shoes	鞋	1-1
心	xīn	*n.* heart, mind	心	1-1
心里	xīnli	in (one's) heart	心裡	2-2
心目中	xīnmùzhōng	*phr.* in one's eyes	心目中	4-1
心情	xīnqíng	*n.* mood	心情	4-1
新潮	xīncháo	*n.* new trend; *adj.* trendy, fashionable	新潮	4-3
新鲜	xīnxiān	*adj.* fresh	新鮮	2-1
行人	xíngrén	*n.* pedestrian	行人	2-1
选	xuǎn	*v.* choose, elect	選	1-1
选择	xuǎnzé	*v.* choose; *n.* option, choice	選擇	3-3
学期	xuéqī	*n.* term, semester	學期	2-1
Y 亚洲	Yàzhōu	*n.* Asia	亞洲	2-3
烟味	yānwèi	*n.* cigarette smell	煙味	3-2
颜色	yánsè	*n.* color	顏色	3-3
眼里	yǎnlǐ	*n.* inside one's eyes	眼裡	4-1
养老院	yǎnglǎoyuàn	*n.* retirement village	養老院	4-1
也好	yěhǎo	*phr.* may as well, may not be a bad idea	也好	3-2
页	yè	*n.* page	頁	1-1
宜人	yírén	*adj.* pleasant, delightful	宜人	2-1
一辈子	yíbèizi	*n.* all one's life, a lifetime	一輩子	4-1
一旦	yídàn	*adv.* once, in case, now that	一旦	4-2
一切	yíqiè	*n.* everything, all	一切	2-3
一边……一边……	yìbiān...yìbiān...	do one thing while doing another	一邊……一邊……	2-2
一生	yìshēng	*n.* all one's life	一生	2-3
一直	yìzhí	*adv.* continuously	一直	3-3
饮茶	yǐnchá	*n.* yum cha - a Cantonese meal of small snacks and tea	飲茶	2-2
印象	yìnxiàng	*n.* impression	印象	2-1
应该	yīnggāi	*v.* should, ought to	應該	1-2, 2-2
赢	yíng	*v.* win; beat	贏	1-2
拥吻	yōngwěn	*n.* hug and kiss	擁吻	3-1
永远	yǒngyuǎn	*adv.* forever	永遠	4-1
用心	yòngxīn	*adj.* attentive, diligent	用心	2-3
优美	yōuměi	*adj.* fine, exquisite	優美	2-1
邮件	yóujiàn	*n.* mail	郵件	1-3

Simplified	Pinyin	English	Traditional	Lesson
邮址	yóuzhǐ	*n.* mail address	郵址	1-3
游戏	yóuxì	*n.* game	遊戲	1-3
游园会	yóuyuánhuì	*n.* fete	遊園會	1-2
犹豫	yóuyù	*v.* hesitate, be indecisive	猶豫	3-3
有朋自远方来	yǒu péng zì yuǎnfāng lái	a friend from afar	有朋自遠方來	2-1
有完没完	yǒu wán méi wán	*colloq.* 'Do you have enough or not?'	有完沒完	4-2
有的	yǒude	*adj.* some, a few	有的	2-2
有点儿	yǒudiǎnr	*adv.* a bit, somewhat	有點兒	1-1
有害	yǒuhài	*adj.* harmful	有害	4-2
有名	yǒumíng	*adj.* famous, renowned	有名	2-3
有时侯	yǒushíhou	*adv.* sometimes	有時候	2-3
友善	yǒushàn	*adj.* friendly	友善	2-1
有学问	yǒuxuéwèn	*adj.* knowledgeable	有學問	2-3
玉红	Yùhóng	*n.* a woman's name	玉紅	2-3
员工	yuángōng	*n.* employee	員工	3-2
远方	yuǎnfāng	*n.* distant place	遠方	2-1
院子	yuànzi	*n.* courtyard	院子	2-3
运动会	yùndònghuì	*n.* sports carnival	運動會	1-2
运气	yùnqì	*n.* luck	運氣	3-2
Z 杂货店	záhuòdiàn	*n.* grocery store	雜貨店	3-2
杂志	zázhì	*n.* magazine	雜誌	2-2
在于	zài yú	*v.* be determined by, depend on	在於	4-2
赞成	zànchéng	*v.* approve of, agree with	贊成	4-1
脏	zāng	*adj.* dirty	髒	3-2
增加	zēngjiā	*v.* add, increase	增加	1-2
章	Zhāng	*n.* a surname; [zhāng] chapter	章	1-1
招	zhāo	*v.* recruit	招	3-1
着急	zháojí	*v.* feel worried	著急	1-3
照顾	zhàogù	*v.* look after, take care of	照顧	3-2
着	zhe	*part.* used to indicate a continuing state, or an action in progress	著	1-2
整个	zhěnggè	*adj.* whole, entire	整個	1-2
挣	zhèng	*v.* earn, make (money)	掙	3-1
正在	zhèngzài	*adv.* in process of (indicates an action is in progress)	正在	1-2
枝	zhī	*m.w.* [for pens, pencils, etc.]	枝	1-1
纸	zhǐ	*n.* paper	紙	2-2
纸箱	zhǐxiāng	*n.* carton	紙箱	2-2
只好	zhǐhǎo	*adv.* have to, have no choice but	只好	3-3
种	zhǒng	*m.w.* kind, type	種	3-2
重视	zhòngshì	*v.* consider important	重視	2-2
壮	zhuàng	*adj.* strong, muscular	壯	4-1
资料	zīliào	*n.* data, information	資料	1-1, 1-3
自己人	zìjǐrén	*n.* one of us, people on one's own side	自己人	2-3
自相矛盾	zìxiāng-máodùn	*idiom.* be self-contradictory	自相矛盾	4-3
自在	zìzai	*adj.* at ease, comfortable	自在	2-2
走走	zǒuzou	*v.* travel around, walk around	走走	2-3
最少	zuìshǎo	*adv.* at least	最少	4-2
座	zuò	*m.w.* [for large and solid thing]	座	2-3
作怪	zuòguài	*v.* act mischievously, create mischief	作怪	4-3

Appendix 2

WORDS AND EXPRESSIONS
English-Chinese

English	Simplified	Pinyin
A		
a bit, somewhat	有点儿	yǒudiǎnr
a few, some	有的	yǒude
accompany, follow	跟	gēn
activity	活动	huódòng
actually, in fact	其实	qíshí
actually, the very end	究竟	jiūjìng
add, increase	增加	zēngjiā
(be) addicted to	上瘾	shàngyǐn
Africa	非洲	Fēizhōu
against, oppose	反对	fǎnduì
air	空气	kōngqì
all, everything	一切	yíqiè
all one's life	一生	yìshēng
all one's life	一辈子	yíbèizi
allow, let; give way	让	ràng
almost	几乎	jīhū
also, in addition	而且	érqiě
although	虽然	suīrán
always, all the time	老是	lǎoshì
and, towards or with	跟	gēn
and so forth, and so on	等	děng
(get) angry, take offence	生气	shēngqì
anyway, anyhow	反正	fǎnzhèng
approve of, agree with	赞成	zànchéng
arrange, set up, place	摆	bǎi
arrogant, conceited	骄傲	jiāo'ào
Asia	亚洲	Yàzhōu
ask or raise a question	发问	fāwèn
at ease, comfortable	自在	zìzai
at ease, stop worrying	放心	fàngxīn
at first, originally	本来	běnlái
at least	最少	zuìshǎo
at that time, then	当时	dāngshí
at the time (when something happens)	临时	línshí
attendant	服务员	fúwùyuán
attentive, diligent	用心	yòngxīn
attitude	态度	tàidù

English	Simplified	Pinyin
B		
bald eagle	秃鹰	tūyīng
barbecue	烤肉	kǎoròu
(take a) bath	洗澡	xǐzǎo
beach, seaside	海边	hǎibiān
beat; win	赢	yíng
(be) beaten; lose	输	shū
beauty salon	美容院	měiróngyuàn
become	成为	chéngwéi
become, turn into	成	chéng
beer	啤酒	píjiǔ
begin, start	开始	kāishǐ
besides; except	除了…以外	chúle...yǐwài
big deal	大不了	dàbùliǎo
bin, bucket, barrel	桶	tǒng
body	身体	shēntǐ
boss	老板	lǎobǎn
bottle, vase	瓶子	píngzi
bowling (tenpin)	保龄球	bǎolìngqiú
box	箱	xiāng
boyfriend	男朋友	nánpéngyou
bread	面包	miànbāo
break up	吹	chuī
break up, part company	分手	fēnshǒu
breakdown (computer)	死机	sǐjī
but	却	què
but, yet, nevertheless	但是	dànshì
C		
can, tin, jar	罐子	guànzi
candidate	人选	rénxuǎn
cannot endure	受不了	shòu bù liǎo
Cantonese meal of small snacks and tea	饮茶	yǐnchá
care about	关心	guānxīn
(be) careful, take care	小心	xiǎoxīn
carton	纸箱	zhǐxiāng
catch up with; hurry	赶	gǎn
CD, DVD or VCD	光盘	guāngpán

English	Simplified	Pinyin
chance, opportunity	机会	jīhuì
change	改	gǎi
charming	迷人	mírén
chat	聊天	liáotiān
chat freely	无所不谈	wú suǒ bù tán
chat room	聊天室	liáotiān shì
chess	国际象棋	guójì xiàngqí
children	小孩	xiǎohái
chocolate	巧克力	qiǎokèlì
choir	合唱团	héchàngtuán
choose, elect	选	xuǎn
choose; option, choice	选择	xuǎnzé
cigarette	香烟	xiāngyān
cigarette smell	烟味	yānwèi
cinema	电影院	diànyǐngyuàn
class leader	班长	bānzhǎng
class meeting	班会	bānhuì
clearly, obviously	明明	míngmíng
clerk, salesperson	店员	diànyuán
climate	气候	qìhòu
club or society of special interest	社	shè
coffee	咖啡	kāfēi
cola	可乐	kělè
color	颜色	yánsè
come over	过来	guòlái
comfortable, at ease	自在	zìzai
complain	抱怨	bàoyuàn
complete; finish	完	wán
computer/video game	电子游戏	diànzǐ yóuxì
conceited, arrogant	骄傲	jiāo'ào
condemn, scold	骂	mà
conservative	保守	bǎoshǒu
consider, think	认为	rènwéi
consider important	重视	zhòngshì
contact, get in touch with	联系	liánxì
continuously	一直	yìzhí
contradictory, in a dilemma	矛盾	máodùn
convenient	方便	fāngbiàn
convenient to use	好用	hǎoyòng
cool (slang)	酷	kù
courtyard	院子	yuànzi
(to) cross, to interact	交	jiāo
cry	哭	kū
customer, client	顾客	gùkè

D

English	Simplified	Pinyin
dance party	舞会	wǔhuì
data, information	资料	zīliào
daydream	白日梦	báirìmèng
decide	决定	juédìng
deep, dark	深	shēn
delicate and pretty	清秀	qīngxiù
delightful, pleasant	宜人	yírén
depend on, determined by	在于	zài yú
deposit, save	存	cún
design	设计	shèjì
die	死掉	sǐdiào
different	不同	bùtóng
difficult, hard	难	nán
(in a) dilemma, contradictory	矛盾	máodùn
diligent, attentive	用心	yòngxīn
dirty	脏	zāng
(in) disorder, messy	乱	luàn
distant place	远方	yuǎnfāng
disturb	打扰	dǎrǎo
disturb, quarrel; noisy	吵	chǎo
do drugs	吸毒	xīdú
do one thing while doing another	一边…… 一边……	yìbiān... yìbiān...
'Do you have enough or not?'	有完没完	yǒu wán méi wán
doze off	打瞌睡	dǎ kēshuì
dress & personal adornment	服饰	fúshì
dress up; style of dress	打扮	dǎbàn
drop it, forget it	算了吧	suànleba
dusk, early evening	傍晚	bàngwǎn
dye	染	rǎn

E

English	Simplified	Pinyin
e-mail	电子邮件	diànzǐ yóujiàn
e-mail address	电子邮址	diànzǐ yóuzhǐ
ear piercing	耳洞	ěrdòng
early evening, dusk	傍晚	bàngwǎn
earn, make (money)	挣	zhèng
earrings	耳环	ěrhuán
easy	容易	róngyì
easy going, not fussy	随便	suíbiàn
egg on, urge	怂恿	sǒngyǒng
either or, or	或	huò
elect, choose	选	xuǎn

English	Simplified	Pinyin
electronic	电子	diànzǐ
employee	员工	yuángōng
empty	空	kōng
enjoy oneself to the full	过瘾	guòyǐn
enter	进	jìn
enthusiastic	热心	rèxīn
environment	环境	huánjìng
environmental protection	环保	huánbǎo
ever, once, formerly	曾经	céngjīng
every region	各地	gèdì
everyday	每天	měitiān
everything, all	一切	yíqiè
everywhere	到处	dàochù
example sentence	例句	lìjù
excellent, good [oral]	棒	bàng
except; besides	除了…以外	chúle...yǐwài
exchange, swap	交换	jiāohuàn
exercise, practice	练习	liànxí
experience	经验	jīngyàn
experience	体验	tǐyàn
exquisite, fine	优美	yōuměi
extracurricular	课外	kèwài
extremely, exceedingly	不得了	bùdéliǎo
extremely, exceedingly	极	jí
extremely, fully, very	十分	shífēn

F

English	Simplified	Pinyin
facsimile	传真	chuánzhēn
famous brand	名牌	míngpái
(in) fashion, popular	流行	liúxíng
fashion shop	服饰店	fúshìdiàn
fashionable; new trend	新潮	xīncháo
fast food	快餐	kuàicān
father	父亲	fùqīn
fatigued, tired	累	lèi
feed	喂	wèi
feel, feeling	感觉	gǎnjué
fete	游园会	yóuyuánhuì
fine, exquisite	优美	yōuměi
fine, good	佳	jiā
finish, complete	完	wán
follow	随	suí
follow, accompany	跟	gēn
forbid, not allow	不准	bùzhǔn
force one's way in or out	闯	chuǎng

English	Simplified	Pinyin
forget it, drop it	算了吧	suànleba
form teacher	班主任	bānzhǔrèn
formerly, once, ever	曾经	céngjīng
fresh	新鲜	xīnxiān
(a) friend from afar	有朋自远方来	yǒu péng zì yuǎnfāng lái
friendly	友善	yǒushàn
(to be) full	饱	bǎo
fully, very, extremely	十分	shífēn
function	功能	gōngnéng
future	将来	jiānglái

G

English	Simplified	Pinyin
game	游戏	yóuxì
garbage, rubbish	垃圾	lājī, lèsè
get along well	谈得来	tán de lái
get in touch with, contact	联系	liánxì
get on the internet	上网	shàng wǎng
giant panda	大熊猫	dàxióngmāo
girl	女孩子	nǚháizi
girlfriend	女朋友	nǚpéngyou
give up, quit	戒	jiè
give way; let, allow	让	ràng
golf	高尔夫球	gāo'ěrfūqiú
good, excellent [oral]	棒	bàng
good, fine	佳	jiā
good-looking	帅	shuài
greet somebody	打招呼	dǎzhāohu
grocery store	杂货店	záhuòdiàn
group, organization	团	tuán
group, team	队	duì
gymnastics	体操	tǐcāo

H

English	Simplified	Pinyin
half dead	半死	bànsǐ
handsome	帅	shuài
happy	高兴	gāoxìng
(feel) happy, rejoice	开心	kāixīn
hard, difficult	难	nán
harmful	有害	yǒuhài
have to, have no choice but	只好	zhǐhǎo
heart, mind	心	xīn
heart set on, be tempted	动心	dòngxīn
heat (v.)	加温	jiāwēn
heated pool	温水游泳池	wēnshuǐ yóuyǒngchí

English	Simplified	Pinyin
help, helpful	帮忙	bāngmáng
hesitate, indecisive	犹豫	yóuyù
hide	藏	cáng
hippopotamus	河马	hémǎ
historic site	古迹	gǔjī
hole	洞	dòng
(have a) holiday/vacation	放假	fàngjià
homeroom teacher	班主任	bānzhǔrèn
(speak out) honestly	老实说来	lǎoshí shuō lái
hoop, ring	环	huán
hope	希望	xīwàng
hospitable	好客	hàokè
hot pot	火锅	huǒguō
housework	家事	jiāshì
hug and kiss	拥吻	yōngwěn
hurry; catch up with	赶	gǎn
hurry up	快点儿	kuàidiǎnr

I

English	Simplified	Pinyin
impression	印象	yìnxiàng
in addition to	除了……以外	chúle...yǐwài
in case, once, now that	一旦	yídàn
in fact, actually	其实	qíshí
in process of	正在	zhèngzài
in the class	班上	bānshàng
in (one's) heart	心里	xīnli
in one's eyes	心目中	xīnmùzhōng
incompatible	不合	bùhé
inconvenient, troublesome	麻烦	máfan
increase, add	增加	zēngjiā
indecisive, hesitate	犹豫	yóuyù
indicative word	把	bǎ
information, data	资料	zīliào
inside one's eyes	眼里	yǎnlǐ
(to) interact, to cross	交	jiāo
internet friend	网友	wǎngyǒu
intolerable	受不了	shòu bù liǎo
item	项目	xiàngmù

J

English	Simplified	Pinyin
jar, tin, can	罐子	guànzi
job, work; to work	工作	gōngzuò
join in	加入	jiārù
just, only just	才	cái
just, so happen that	刚好	gānghǎo

K

English	Simplified	Pinyin
kangaroo	袋鼠	dàshǔ
karate	空手道	kōngshǒudào
kebab	肉串	ròuchuàn
kind, type	种	zhǒng
kind-hearted	善良	shànliáng
kiwi bird	奇异鸟	qíyìniǎo
koala	考拉	kǎolā
	树熊	shùxióng
	无尾熊	wúwěixióng

L

English	Simplified	Pinyin
let, allow; give way	让	ràng
let know, tell	告诉	gàosù
level, standard	水平	shuǐpíng
liberal, open-minded	开通	kāitōng
lie (n.)	谎	huǎng
(to tell) lie	说谎	shuōhuǎng
(a) lifetime	一辈子	yíbèizi
listless, sluggish	懒洋洋	lǎnyángyáng
local; location, place	地方	dìfāng
local conditions and customs	风土人情	fēngtǔrénqíng
look after	照顾	zhàogù
lose; be beaten	输	shū
lose; throw	丢	diū
lost in thought	发呆	fādāi
love (romantic)	爱情	àiqíng
love, be in love	恋爱	liàn'ài
low	低	dī
luck	运气	yùnqì
lung cancer	肺癌	fèi'ái

M

English	Simplified	Pinyin
m.w. - letter	封	fēng
m.w. - cigarette	根	gēn
m.w. - package	包	bāo
m.w. - work, newspaper, magazine	份	fèn
m.w. - pens, pencils	枝	zhī
m.w. - car, bus, bicycle, etc.	辆	liàng
magazine	杂志	zázhì
mail	邮件	yóujiàn
mail address	邮址	yóuzhǐ

English	Simplified	Pinyin
make a mountain out of a molehill	小题大做	xiǎotí-dàzuò
make trouble	捣蛋	dǎodàn
make use of, use	利用	lìyòng
Mandarin	普通话	pǔtōnghuà
marry, get married	结婚	jiéhūn
material (fabric)	料子	liàozi
may as well, may not be a bad idea	也好	yěhǎo
maybe, perhaps	说不定	shuōbúdìng
meet, see	见面	jiànmiàn
messy, in disorder	乱	luàn
mind, heart	心	xīn
(act) mischievously	作怪	zuòguài
mood	心情	xīnqíng
mother	母亲	mǔqīn
mostly	多半	duōbàn
moving, touching	感人	gǎnrén
muscular, strong	壮	zhuàng
music store	唱片行	chàngpiànháng

N

English	Simplified	Pinyin
nag	唠叨	láodao
navel	肚脐	dùqí
navel piercing	肚脐洞	dùqídòng
navel ring	肚脐环	dùqíhuán
nearby, in the vicinity	附近	fùjìn
nevertheless, but, yet	但是	dànshì
new trend; trendy	新潮	xīncháo
new word	生词	shēngcí
newsboy	送报员	sòngbàoyuán
newspaper	报纸	bàozhǐ
noisy; disturb	吵	chǎo
North America	北美洲	Běiměizhōu
not allow, forbid	不准	bùzhǔn
not fussy, easy going	随便	suíbiàn
not only	不但	búdàn
nothing more, that's all	而已	éryǐ
novel	小说	xiǎoshuō
now that, once, in case	一旦	yídàn

O

English	Simplified	Pinyin
obviously, clearly	明明	míngmíng
odd, strange, weird	怪怪的	guàiguàide
odor, smell	味	wèi

English	Simplified	Pinyin
(take) offence, get angry	生气	shēngqì
Oh my God!	我的天	wǒ de tiān
old fogey	老古板	lǎogǔbǎn
on one's body	身上	shēnshàng
once, formerly, ever	曾经	céngjīng
once, in case, now that	一旦	yídàn
one of us, people on one's own side	自己人	zìjǐrén
open-minded, liberal	开通	kāitōng
opportunity, chance	机会	jīhuì
oppose, against	反对	fǎnduì
option, choice; choose	选择	xuǎnzé
or, either or	或	huò
organization, group	团	tuán
originally, at first	本来	běnlái
other people	别人	biérén
ought to, should	应该	yīnggāi

P

English	Simplified	Pinyin
page	页	yè
paper	纸	zhǐ
parents	父母亲	fùmǔqīn
park	公园	gōngyuán
part company, break up	分手	fēnshǒu
(have a) part-time job	打工	dǎgōng
passive smoking	二手烟	èrshǒuyān
pay	付	fù
peculiar	特有	tèyǒu
pedestrian	行人	xíngrén
people on on one's own side, one of us	自己人	zìjǐrén
perform an act	表演	biǎoyǎn
perhaps, maybe	说不定	shuōbúdìng
pierce, penerate	穿	chuān
(it's a) pity, too bad	可惜	kěxī
place, location	地方	dìfāng
plastic bag	塑料袋	sùliàodài
pleasant, delightful	宜人	yírén
pocket money	零花钱	línghuāqián
popular (person)	出风头	chūfēngtóu
popular, in fashion	流行	liúxíng
popularity	人缘儿	rényuánr
portable listening device	随声听	suíshēngtīng
practice, exercise	练习	liànxí
practise	练	liàn

English-Chinese

English	Simplified	Pinyin
price	价钱	jiàqián
prince charming	白马王子	báimǎ-wángzǐ
problem, shortcoming	毛病	máobìng
protect; protection	保护	bǎohù
put in order, tidy up	收拾	shōushi

Q

English	Simplified	Pinyin
quarrel; noisy	吵	chǎo
quarrel	吵架	chǎojià
quit	戒掉	jièdiào
quit, give up	戒	jiè
quit, resign, sack	辞	cí
quit smoking	戒烟	jièyān

R

English	Simplified	Pinyin
really	实在	shízài
recruit	招	zhāo
recycle	回收	huíshōu
regard as; treat as	当	dàng
rejoice, happy	开心	kāixīn
relations with people	人缘儿	rényuánr
relaxed	轻松	qīngsōng
resign, sack, quit	辞	cí
restaurant	餐馆	cānguǎn
restrict, restrain	拘束	jūshù
return, reward	回报	huíbào
return (things)	退	tuì
ring, hoop	环	huán
roomy, spacious	宽敞	kuānchang
row; rowing	划船	huáchuán
rubbish, garbage	垃圾	lājī, lèsè
rush	闯	chuǎng

S

English	Simplified	Pinyin
sack, resign, quit	辞	cí
sad	难过	nánguò
salad	沙拉	shālā
salary, wage	工资	gōngzī
salesperson, clerk	店员	diànyuán
sausage	香肠	xiāngcháng
save, deposit	存	cún
say as you please	随你怎么说	suí nǐ zěnme shuō
scenery	风景	fēngjǐng
school starts	开学	kāixué
scold, condemn	骂	mà

English	Simplified	Pinyin
seashore, beach	海边	hǎibiān
see, meet	见面	jiànmiàn
self-contradictory	自相矛盾	zìxiāng-máodùn
semester, term	学期	xúeqī
serve as, work as	当	dāng
set up, arrange, place	摆	bǎi
shine upon	晒	shài
shoes	鞋	xié
shop, store	店	diàn
shortcoming, problem	毛病	máobìng
should, ought to	应该	yīnggāi
show off	出风头	chūfēngtóu
skin cancer	皮肤癌	pífū'ái
slow	慢	màn
sluggish, listless	懒洋洋	lǎnyángyáng
smell (v.)	闻	wén
smell, odor	味	wèi
smoke (cigarette)	抽	chōu
smoke (v.)	吸烟	xīyān
snack	小吃	xiǎochī
so happen that, just	刚好	gānghǎo
softball	垒球	lěiqiú
solar energy	太阳能	tàiyángnéng
some, a few	有的	yǒude
sometimes	有时侯	yǒushíhou
somewhat, a bit	有点儿	yǒudiǎnr
sound; voice	声	shēng
spacious, roomy	宽敞	kuānchang
speak, talk	讲话	jiǎnghuà
spend	花	huā
spend pocket money	零花	línghuā
sports carnival	运动会	yùndònghuì
spring holiday	春假	chūnjià
stand, stall	摊位	tānwèi
standard, level	水平	shuǐpíng
stare blankly	发呆	fādāi
start, begin	开始	kāishǐ
startle (someone)	吓一跳	xià yí tiào
steak	牛排	niúpái
stop worrying, at ease	放心	fàngxīn
story, tale	故事	gùshì
strange, odd, weird	怪怪的	guàiguàide
stroll around the street	逛街	guàngjiē
strong, muscular	壮	zhuàng
study	念	niàn

English	Simplified	Pinyin
style	式样	shìyàng
style of dress; dress up	打扮	dǎbàn
succeed, success	成功	chénggōng
suggest	提议	tíyì
sun	太阳	tàiyáng
swap, exchange	交换	jiāohuàn
symphony	交响乐	jiāoxiǎngyuè

T

English	Simplified	Pinyin
take a picture	拍照	pāizhào
take care, be careful	小心	xiǎoxīn
take care of	照顾	zhàogù
tale, story	故事	gùshì
talk, speak	讲话	jiǎnghuà
tattoo	文身	wénshēn
team, group	队	duì
tell, let know	告诉	gàosù
temper	脾气	píqi
tempted, heart set on	动心	dòngxīn
term, semester	学期	xuéqī
that's all, nothing more	而已	éryǐ
then, at that time	当时	dāngshí
think, consider	认为	rènwéi
throw; lose	丢	diū
throw up, vomit	吐	tù
tidy up, put in order	收拾	shōushi
tin, can, jar	罐子	guànzi
tired, fatigued	累	lèi
too bad, it's a pity	可惜	kěxī
touching, moving	感人	gǎnrén
tourist group	旅行团	lǚxíngtuán
towards, with	跟	gēn
traffic	交通	jiāotōng
(have a) traffic jam	堵车	dǔchē
travel around	走走	zǒuzou
treat as; regard as	当	dàng
trendy; new trend	新潮	xīncháo
troublesome, inconvenient	麻烦	máfan
try on (clothes/shoes)	试穿	shìchuān
turn into, become	成	chéng
turn over	翻	fān
(private) tutor	家教	jiājiào
type, kind	种	zhǒng

U

English	Simplified	Pinyin
unbearable	受不了	shòu bù liǎo
understand, understanding	了解	liǎojiě
upper garment	上衣	shàngyī
urge, egg on	怂恿	sǒngyǒng
use, make use of	利用	lìyòng
(get) used to	习惯	xíguàn

V

English	Simplified	Pinyin
various kinds	各种	gèzhǒng
vase, bottle	瓶子	píngzi
very, fully, extremely	十分	shífēn
(in the) vicinity, nearby	附近	fùjìn
voice; sound	声	shēng
volleyball	排球	páiqiú
vomit, throw up	吐	tù

W

English	Simplified	Pinyin
wage, salary	工资	gōngzī
walk around	走走	zǒuzou
waste, wasteful	浪费	làngfèi
wear (clothes, shoes)	穿	chuān
wear (hat, ring)	戴	dài
web page	网页	wǎngyè
website	网址	wǎngzhǐ
weird, strange, odd	怪怪的	guàiguàide
well-known scenic spot	名胜	míngshèng
(the) West	西方	xīfāng
when in Rome, do as the Romans do	入乡随俗	rù xiāng suí sú
wife (formal term)	妻子	qīzi
win; beat	赢	yíng
window-shopping	逛街	guàngjiē
with, towards	跟	gēn
work as, serve as	当	dāng
work, job; to work	工作	gōngzuò
world	世界	shìjiè
(feel) worried	着急	zháojí
wrap (v.)	包	bāo

Y

English	Simplified	Pinyin
yet, but, nevertheless	但是	dànshì
young people	年轻人	niánqīng rén

Z

English	Simplified	Pinyin
zoo	动物园	dòngwùyuán

Appendix 3

LIST OF RADICALS
部首目录

This chart is based on the 汉字部首表 *The Table of Indexing Chinese Character Component*, 2009.
Names and meanings of radicals are added to assist learning.

① 一	丨 亅	丿	丶	乛	② 十	厂 厂	匚	卜 卜
(héng) (horizontal)	(shù) (vertical)	(piě) (left stroke)	(diǎn) (dot)	(zhé) (fold)	shí ten	chǎng mill	fāng basket	bǔ to predict
冂 冂	八 丷	人 亻 入	勹	儿	匕	几 凡	亠	冫
jiōng borders	bā eight	rén people	bāo to wrap	ér child	bǐ ancient spoon	jī table	tóu head	bīng ice
冖	凵	卩 㔾	刀 刂 ⺈	力	又	厶	廴	③ 干
mì to cover	gǎn rice container	jié to control	dāo knife	lì strength	yòu also, again	sī private	yǐn long walk	gān dry
工	土 士	艹 艸	寸	廾	大	尢 尢 尣	弋	小 ⺌
gōng work	tǔ soil	cǎo grass	cùn inch	gǒng to join hands	dà big	wāng lame	yì ancient arrow	xiǎo little
口	囗	山	巾	彳	彡	夕	夂	爿 丬
kǒu mouth	wéi to enclose	shān mountain	jīn cloth	chì slow walk	shān hairy	xì evening	suī leisure walk	qiáng plank
广	门 門	宀	辶 辵	彐 彑 彐	尸	己 巳 巴	弓	子
guǎng vast	mén door	mián house	chuò abrupt walk	jì pig's head	shī corpse	jǐ self	gōng bow	zǐ son
屮 屮	女	飞 飛	马 馬	幺	巛	④ 王 玉	无 旡	韦 韋
chè to burgeon	nǚ female	fēi to fly	mǎ horse	yāo tiny	chuān river	wáng/yù king/jade	wú nothing	wéi leather
木 朩	支	犬 犭	歹 歺	车 轧 車	牙	戈	比	瓦
mù tree	zhī branch	quǎn dog	dǎi evil	chē vehicle	yá tooth	gē spear	bǐ to compare	wǎ tile
止	攴 攵	日 曰	贝 貝	水 氵 氺	见 見	牛 牜	手 扌 龵	气
zhǐ to stop	pū to tap	rì sun	bèi shell	shuǐ water	jiàn to see	niú ox, cow	shǒu hand	qì air
毛	长 镸 長	片	斤	爪 爫	父	月 ⺆	氏	欠
máo hair	cháng long	piàn slice	jīn axe	zhuǎ claw	fù father	yuè moon	shì clan	qiàn to owe
风 風	殳	文	方	火 灬	斗	户	心 忄 ⺗	毋 母
fēng wind	shū a weapon	wén literature	fāng square	huǒ fire	dǒu a container	hù door	xīn heart	wú do not

⑤ 示 礻 shì to show	甘 gān sweet	石 shí stone	龙 龍 lóng dragon	业 yè business	目 mù eye	田 tián field	罒 wǎng net	皿 mǐn shallow container
生 shēng to give birth	矢 shǐ arrow	禾 hé crop	白 bái white	瓜 guā melon	鸟 鳥 niǎo bird	疒 chuáng illness	立 lì to stand	穴 xuè cave
疋 ⻊ pǐ roll of cloth	皮 pí skin	癶 bō heel to heel	矛 máo spear	⑥ 耒 lěi plough	老 耂 lǎo old	耳 ěr ear	臣 chén officer	西 覀 襾 yà to cover
而 ér and yet	页 頁 yè page	至 zhì to reach	虍 虎 hǔ tiger	虫 chóng insect	肉 ròu meat	缶 fǒu jar	舌 shé tongue	竹 ⺮ zhú bamboo
臼 jiù mortar	自 zì self	血 xiě blood	舟 zhōu boat	色 sè color	齐 齊 qí aligned	衣 礻 yī clothes	羊 ⺶ ⺷ yáng sheep	米 mǐ rice
聿 ⺻ ⺼ yù writing instrument	艮 gěn hard	羽 yǔ feather	糸 纟 糹 mì silk	⑦ 麦 麥 mài wheat	走 zǒu to walk	赤 chì red	豆 dòu bean	酉 yǒu wine
辰 chén time	豕 shǐ pig	卤 鹵 lǔ to stew	里 lǐ inside	足 ⻊ zú foot	邑 阝 (right) yì town	身 shēn body	釆 biàn to separate	谷 gǔ valley
豸 zhì leg-less reptile	龟 龜 guī tortoise	角 jiǎo horn	言 讠 yán speech	辛 xīn peppery	⑧ 青 qīng green	卓 gàn morning sun	雨 yǔ rain	非 fēi not
齿 齒 chǐ tooth	黾 黽 mǐn to strive	隹 zhuī bird	阜 阝 (left) fù mound	金 钅 jīn metals	鱼 魚 yú fish	隶 lì subordinate	⑨ 革 gé leather	面 miàn face
韭 jiǔ chives	骨 gǔ bone	香 xiāng fragrant	鬼 guǐ ghost	食 饣 亻 shí food	音 yīn sound	首 shǒu head	⑩ 髟 biāo long hair	鬲 lì cauldron
鬥 dòu to fight	高 gāo tall	⑪ 黄 huáng yellow	麻 má flax	鹿 lù deer	⑫ 鼎 dǐng cooking vessel	黑 hēi black	黍 shǔ millet	⑬ 鼓 gǔ drum
鼠 shǔ rodent	⑭ 鼻 bí nose	⑰ 龠 yuè type of flute						

Appendix 4

CHARACTERS LEARNT IN 你好 1–4

(Characters learnt in this book are displayed in purple.)

Chinese (Radical)	Pinyin	English

1 Stroke

| 一 (一) | yī | one (1-3) |

2 Strokes

二 (一)	èr	two (1-3)
七 (一)	qī	seven (1-3)
九 (丿)	jiǔ	nine (1-3)
了 (乙)	le, liǎo	[grammatical word] (2-2)
十 (十)	shí	ten (1-3)
八 (八)	bā	eight (1-3)
人 (人)	rén	people, person (1-1)
儿 (儿)	ér	[word ending]; son (2-3)
几 (几)	jǐ	how many (1-4)
又 (又)	yòu	and, again (3-9)

3 Strokes

三 (一)	sān	three (1-3)
下 (一)	xià	under, down (2-2)
才 (一)	cái	just, only just (4-1)
久 (丿)	jiǔ	long (of time) (3-2)
也 (乙)	yě	also, too (1-8)
习 (乙)	xí	to practise (3-2)
千 (十)	qiān	thousand (3-2)
上 (卜)	shàng	to go to, to attend; up (1-10)
个 (人)	gè	[measure word] (1-6)
么 (厶)	me	[word ending] (1-5)
工 (工)	gōng	work, job (4-3)
大 (大)	dà	big (1-7)
小 (小)	xiǎo	little (1-7)
口 (口)	kǒu	mouth (1-1)
山 (山)	shān	mountain (1-1)

Chinese (Radical)	Pinyin	English
己 (己)	jǐ	oneself (4-1)
已 (己)	yǐ	already (3-7)
子 (子)	zi; zǐ	[word ending]; child (2-3)
女 (女)	nǚ	woman, female (3-2)
飞 (飞)	fēi	to fly (3-7)
马 (马)	mǎ	horse (1-7)

4 Strokes

五 (一)	wǔ	five (1-3)
开 (一)	kāi	to hold, to open, to start (3-9)
不 (一)	bù	no, not (1-5)
中 (丨)	zhōng	center, middle (1-8)
内 (丨)	nèi	inside (3-6)
为 (丶)	wèi	for (2-8)
书 (乛)	shū	book (2-2)
午 (丿)	wǔ	noon, midday (2-2)
厌 (厂)	yàn	to detest (3-1)
反 (厂)	fǎn	oppose; opposite (4-4)
公 (八)	gōng	public (3-3)
分 (八)	fēn	minute; cent (2-2)
什 (亻)	shén	what (1-5)
从 (人)	cóng	from, since (4-3)
以 (人)	yǐ	so as to (2-7)
今 (人)	jīn	present (time) (2-1)
六 (亠)	liù	six (1-3)
认 (讠)	rèn	to recognize (4-1)
切 (刀)	qiè	to cut (4-2)
友 (又)	yǒu	friend (1-10)
太 (大)	tài	too, excessively (2-4)
天 (大)	tiān	day; sky (2-1)
少 (小)	shǎo	few, little (2-6)
车 (车)	chē	car, vehicle (2-3)

Chinese (Radical)	Pinyin	English
比（比）	bǐ	to compare; (more) than (3-4)
日（日）	rì	day; sun (2-1)
水（水）	shuǐ	water (3-8)
见（见）	jiàn	to see (3-6)
手（手）	shǒu	hand (3-7)
牛（牛）	niú	ox, cow (4-2)
毛（毛）	máo	10-cent unit; fur (2-6)
气（气）	qì	air (2-8)
长（长）	cháng; zhǎng	long; to grow (3-3)
片（片）	piàn; piān	thin piece or slice; film (3-7)
父（父）	fù	father (4-2)
月（月）	yuè	month; the moon (2-1)
风（风）	fēng	wind (2-9)
方（方）	fāng	direction (3-7)
火（火）	huǒ	fire (3-3)
心（心）	xīn	heart (4-1)

5 Strokes

Chinese (Radical)	Pinyin	English
世（一）	shì	world (4-2)
本（一）	běn	[m.w. for books etc.] (3-2)
东（一）	dōng	east (3-3)
平（一）	píng	flat (2-8)
且（一）	qiě	also (4-3)
电（丨）	diàn	electricity (2-7)
乐（丿）	lè; yuè	happy, joyful; music (2-1)
半（丶）	bàn	half (2-2)
用（冂）	yòng	to use (4-1)
他（亻）	tā	he, him (1-2)
们（亻）	men	[plural word] (1-2)
包（勹）	bāo	to wrap; bag (4-4)
北（丨）	běi	north (2-9)
写（冖）	xiě	to write (2-2)
讨（讠）	tǎo	to incur (3-1)
让（讠）	ràng	let, to allow (4-3)
出（凵）	chū	to go/come out (4-4)

Chinese (Radical)	Pinyin	English
印（卩）	yìn	to print; seal (4-2)
加（力）	jiā	to add (3-7)
对（又）	duì	right, correct (2-1)
发（又）	fā; fà	to emit, to send out; hair (3-8)
去（土）	qù	to go (1-9)
左（工）	zuǒ	left (location) (2-3)
功（工）	gōng	merit; effort (4-1)
节（艹）	jié	section; festival (3-1)
头（大）	tóu	head (3-8)
只（口）	zhī	[m.w. for dogs, cats, birds] (1-7)
右（口）	yòu	right (location) (2-3)
可（口）	kě	may, be permitted (2-7)
号（口）	hào	date; number (2-1)
叫（口）	jiào	to be called, call (1-10)
叨（口）	dāo	talkative (4-3)
四（囗）	sì	four (1-3)
外（夕）	wài	outside (2-3)
冬（夂）	dōng	winter (2-9)
处（夂）	chù	place (4-4)
它（宀）	tā	it (4-2)
边（辶）	biān	[word ending - location]; side (2-3)
末（木）	mò	end (3-4)
正（止）	zhèng	straight, exact (4-1)
汉（氵）	hàn	name of a Chinese dynasty (1-8)
打（扌）	dǎ	to hit, to play (tennis...etc.) (1-9)
礼（礻）	lǐ	courtesy, ritual (3-9)
母（母）	mǔ	mother (4-2)
业（业）	yè	course of study, business (3-2)
生（生）	shēng	to be born, to give birth to; pupil (2-1)
白（白）	bái; Bái	white; a surname (2-4)

6 Strokes

Chinese (Radical)	Pinyin	English
再（一）	zài	again (2-7)
年（丿）	nián	year (1-10)
买（一）	mǎi	to buy (2-6)

Characters learnt

Chinese (Radical)	Pinyin	English
后 (厂)	hòu	behind, after (2-3)
同 (冂)	tóng	same; together (1-10)
网 (冂)	wǎng	net (4-1)
共 (八)	gòng	together (2-6)
关 (丷)	guān	to close (4-1)
件 (亻)	jiàn	[m.w. for clothes] (2-4)
份 (亻)	fèn	[m.w. for job, newspaper...] (4-3)
会 (人)	huì	can, be able to (1-8)
先 (儿)	xiān	first (2-4)
交 (亠)	jiāo	to hand in (3-2)
决 (冫)	jué	to decide (4-4)
次 (冫)	cì	time (frequency) (3-8)
阴 (阝)	yīn	cloudy (2-9)
那 (阝)	nà	that (1-5)
刚 (刂)	gāng	just now, just (4-3)
动 (力)	dòng	to move (1-9)
欢 (又)	huān	happy (1-9)
地 (土)	dì	land, ground (3-7)
场 (土)	chǎng	[m.w. for shows]; field (3-4)
在 (土)	zài	[in progress]; at, in, on (2-2)
当 (⺌)	dāng	to be, to serve as (4-1)
吗 (口)	ma	[question word] (1-5)
吃 (口)	chī	to eat (1-11)
向 (口)	xiàng	towards, to (3-6)
回 (囗)	huí	to return (2-7)
因 (囗)	yīn	cause (2-8)
岁 (山)	suì	year of age (1-4)
师 (巾)	shī	teacher (1-4)
行 (彳)	xíng	to go; OK (2-1)
多 (夕)	duō	many, much (2-6)
名 (夕)	míng	famous; name (4-3)
各 (夂)	gè	every, each (4-2)
安 (宀)	ān	peace, peaceful (3-7)
字 (宀)	zì	character, word (2-2)
过 (辶)	guò	to pass, to cross (3-3)
好 (女)	hǎo	good (1-2)
她 (女)	tā	she, her (1-4)
妈 (女)	mā	mother (1-6)

Chinese (Radical)	Pinyin	English
如 (女)	rú	if (3-6)
红 (纟)	hóng	red (2-4)
级 (纟)	jí	grade, level (1-10)
机 (木)	jī	machine (3-7)
死 (歹)	sǐ	die; death (4-4)
成 (戈)	chéng	to become (4-1)
收 (攵)	shōu	to receive, to collect (3-9)
早 (日)	zǎo	morning, early (2-2)
有 (月)	yǒu	to have, there is/are (1-6)
忙 (忄)	máng	busy (4-1)
百 (白)	bǎi	hundred (3-2)
老 (老)	lǎo	old (1-4)
考 (老)	kǎo	to take/give a test (3-1)
西 (西)	xī	west (3-3)
而 (而)	ér	yet (4-3)
肉 (肉)	ròu	meat (4-2)
自 (自)	zì	self (3-3)
色 (色)	sè	color (2-4)
衣 (衣)	yī	clothes (2-4)
米 (米)	mǐ	uncooked rice (2-8)

7 Strokes

Chinese (Radical)	Pinyin	English
两 (一)	liǎng	two (1-4)
来 (一)	lái	to come (2-7)
更 (一)	gèng	even, even more (2-6)
医 (匚)	yī	doctor, medicine (3-8)
弟 (丷)	dì	younger brother (1-6)
体 (亻)	tǐ	body (4-4)
但 (亻)	dàn	but (4-1)
作 (亻)	zuò	to do (3-2)
你 (亻)	nǐ	you (1-2)
住 (亻)	zhù	to live, to reside (3-3)
位 (亻)	wèi	[m.w. for person]; location (4-2)
冷 (冫)	lěng	cold (2-9)
诉 (讠)	sù	tell; appeal to (4-2)
邮 (阝)	yóu	mail (4-1)
别 (刂)	bié	don't (3-4)
块 (土)	kuài	dollar (oral) (2-6)

Chinese (Radical)	Pinyin	English
坏 (土)	huài	bad; to go bad (3-8)
坐 (土)	zuò	to sit, to board (3-3)
花 (艹)	huā	to spend; flower (4-3)
寿 (寸)	shòu	longevity (3-9)
员 (口)	yuán	personnel (4-3)
听 (口)	tīng	to listen, to hear (4-1)
吧 (口)	ba	[suggestion word] (1-9)
告 (口)	gào	inform (4-2)
吹 (口)	chuī	to blow (4-4)
园 (囗)	yuán	garden (4-2)
希 (巾)	xī	to hope (4-2)
条 (夂)	tiáo	strip; [m.w. for long and thin object] (4-3)
饭 (饣)	fàn	cooked rice, meal (1-11)
应 (广)	yīng	should (4-1)
间 (门)	jiān	[measure word for room] (2-3)
完 (宀)	wán	finish (4-4)
这 (辶)	zhè	this (1-5)
还 (辶)	hái	also, still (2-6)
进 (辶)	jìn	to enter (4-3)
运 (辶)	yùn	to transport; luck (1-9)
迟 (辶)	chí	late (3-2)
远 (辶)	yuǎn	far (3-3)
近 (辶)	jìn	near, close (3-3)
张 (弓)	zhāng; [m.w. for paper]; Zhāng a surname (3-4)
我 (戈)	wǒ	I, me (1-2)
时 (日)	shí	time, hour (2-7)
没 (氵)	méi	[negative word] (1-7)
汽 (氵)	qì	steam (3-3)
护 (扌)	hù	to protect (4-2)
找 (扌)	zhǎo	to look for; to give change (2-7)
把 (扌)	bǎ	[indicative word] (4-1)
报 (扌)	bào	to report; newspaper (4-3)
肚 (月)	dù	abdomen (3-8)
忘 (心)	wàng	to forget (3-2)
快 (忄)	kuài	fast, soon (2-1)
每 (母)	měi	every, each (4-1)

Chinese (Radical)	Pinyin	English
男 (田)	nán	man, male (3-2)
纸 (纟)	zhǐ	paper (4-3)
利 (禾)	lì	sharp; smoothly; to benefit (4-1)
走 (走)	zǒu	to walk, to go (3-3)
里 (里)	lǐ	inside (2-3)
身 (身)	shēn	body (4-4)

8 Strokes

Chinese (Radical)	Pinyin	English
事 (一)	shì	matter, thing, business (2-7)
果 (丨)	guǒ	fruit; result (3-6)
卖 (十)	mài	to sell (2-6)
直 (十)	zhí	straight (4-3)
周 (冂)	zhōu	week (3-4)
其 (八)	qí	that, such (4-4)
京 (亠)	jīng	capital (2-9)
话 (讠)	huà	speech (2-7)
该 (讠)	gāi	should (4-1)
试 (讠)	shì	test, to try (3-1)
参 (厶)	cān	to participate (3-7)
英 (艹)	yīng	elite, brave (1-8)
奇 (大)	qí	unusual (4-4)
呢 (口)	ne	[question word] (2-3)
国 (囗)	guó	nation (1-8)
往 (彳)	wǎng	towards, to (3-3)
备 (田)	bèi	to prepare (3-1)
店 (广)	diàn	shop (4-3)
空 (宀)	kòng	free time (2-7)
宜 (宀)	yí	suitable (2-6)
宠 (宀)	chǒng	to spoil (1-7)
定 (宀)	dìng	to set (4-3)
实 (宀)	shí	fact, real (4-4)
学 (子)	xué	to study, to learn (1-10)
姓 (女)	xìng	family name (4-1)
姐 (女)	jiě	elder sister (1-6)
妹 (女)	mèi	younger sister (1-6)
经 (纟)	jīng	to pass through (3-7)
玩 (王)	wán	to play, to have fun (3-7)
现 (王)	xiàn	now, present (2-2)

Chinese (Radical)	Pinyin	English
环 (王)	huán	to surround; ring, hoop (4-2)
狗 (犭)	gǒu	dog (1-7)
或 (戈)	huò	or (4-3)
些 (止)	xiē	[m.w] a few, some (3-7)
明 (日)	míng	bright (light) (2-1)
易 (日)	yì	easy (4-4)
泳 (氵)	yǒng	swim (4-2)
物 (牛)	wù	object, thing (1-7)
受 (爫)	shòu	to bear; to receive (4-3)
爸 (父)	bà	father (1-6)
服 (月)	fú	clothes (2-4)
朋 (月)	péng	friend (1-10)
放 (攵)	fàng	to put, to let go (4-1)
所 (户 / 斤)	suǒ	so; place (2-8)
炒 (火)	chǎo	to stir-fry (2-8)
性 (忄)	xìng	nature, character (3-6)
怪 (忄)	guài	odd, strange (4-4)
视 (礻)	shì	sight, to look at (3-4)
知 (矢)	zhī	to know (3-1)
和 (禾)	hé	and (1-10)
的 (白)	de	[possessive particle] (1-5)
到 (至)	dào	to go to, to arrive; to (3-2)
房 (方)	fáng	room, house (2-3)
雨 (雨)	yǔ	rain (2-9)
非 (非)	fēi	not, un- (4-1)

9 Strokes

Chinese (Radical)	Pinyin	English
南 (十)	nán	south (3-3)
点 (灬)	diǎn	o'clock; dot; to point (2-2)
前 (丷)	qián	front, before (2-3)
便 (亻)	pián; biàn	cheap; convenience (2-6)
信 (亻)	xìn	letter (mail) (3-9)
保 (亻)	bǎo	to keep, to protect (4-2)
亲 (亠)	qīn	related by blood (4-2)
说 (讠)	shuō	to speak, to say (1-8)
语 (讠)	yǔ	language (1-8)
除 (阝)	chú	except, besides (4-1)

Chinese (Radical)	Pinyin	English
城 (土)	chéng	town (2-8)
茶 (艹)	chá	tea (2-8)
药 (艹)	yào	medicine (3-8)
封 (寸)	fēng	[m.w. for letter] (4-2)
哪 (口)	nǎ	where; which; what (2-3)
虽 (口)	suī	although (4-1)
帮 (巾)	bāng	to help, to assist (4-1)
带 (巾)	dài	to take, to bring (3-7)
很 (彳)	hěn	very (1-7)
饼 (饣)	bǐng	biscuit, cake (3-9)
饺 (饣)	jiǎo	dumpling (gold ingot-shaped) (3-9)
穿 (穴)	chuān	to wear (2-4)
客 (宀)	kè	guest (2-8)
室 (宀)	shì	room (4-1)
送 (辶)	sòng	to give sth. as present (3-9)
迷 (辶)	mí	fan; to lose one's way (3-4)
孩 (子)	hái	child (4-4)
给 (纟)	gěi	to give (2-6)
相 (木)	xiàng	appearance, photo (3-7)
轻 (车)	qīng	light (in weight) (4-4)
是 (日)	shì	is, am, are (1-2)
昨 (日)	zuó	yesterday (2-1)
星 (日)	xīng	star (2-1)
春 (日)	chūn	spring (2-9)
冒 (冂)	mào	to emit, to risk (3-8)
贵 (贝)	guì	expensive, dear (2-6)
活 (氵)	huó	to live; alive (4-1)
觉 (见)	jué; jiào	to feel; sleep (3-6)
拾 (扌)	shí	to pick up (4-2)
挣 (扌)	zhèng	to earn (4-3)
看 (手)	kàn	to read, to see, to watch (2-2)
胖 (月)	pàng	fat, plump (3-6)
怎 (心)	zěn	how (2-4)
祝 (礻)	zhù	to wish (offer good wishes) (3-5)
界 (田)	jiè	boundary (4-2)
思 (田)	sī	to think (3-4)
种 (禾)	zhǒng	kind, type (4-2)

Chinese (Radical)	Pinyin	English
科 (禾)	kē	science (3-1)
秋 (禾)	qiū	autumn, fall (2-9)
要 (西)	yào	to want, would like (2-6)
差 (羊)	chà	not good; differ (3-1)
美 (兰)	měi	beautiful, to beautify (4-4)
面 (面)	miàn	[word ending - location]; face; wheat flour (2-3)
音 (音)	yīn	sound (3-4)

10 Strokes

Chinese (Radical)	Pinyin	English
哥 (一)	gē	elder brother (1-6)
真 (十)	zhēn	really (1-11)
借 (亻)	jiè	to borrow (4-4)
候 (亻)	hòu	time (2-7)
高 (高)	gāo	tall; high (3-6)
离 (亠)	lí	away from (3-3)
凉 (冫)	liáng	cool (2-9)
准 (冫)	zhǔn	standard (3-1)
课 (讠)	kè	lesson, subject (3-1)
请 (讠)	qǐng	please; to invite (2-7)
谁 (讠)	shéi	who (1-4)
谈 (讠)	tán	to talk (4-1)
都 (阝)	dōu	all (2-8)
部 (阝)	bù	[m.w. for films]; part (3-4)
能 (厶)	néng	can, to be able to (3-8)
难 (又)	nán	difficult (4-4)
唠 (口)	láo	talkative (4-3)
夏 (夂)	xià	summer (2-9)
饿 (饣)	è	hungry (1-11)
家 (宀)	jiā	home (1-6)
害 (宀)	hài	harm (4-4)
容 (宀)	róng	to contain; appearance (4-4)
通 (辶)	tōng	to get through (4-2)
逛 (辶)	guàng	to stroll (4-4)
班 (王)	bān	class (3-2)
校 (木)	xiào	school (3-2)
样 (木)	yàng	appearance (2-4)
哭 (犬)	kū	cry (4-4)

Chinese (Radical)	Pinyin	English
较 (车)	jiào	to compare, relatively (3-6)
流 (氵)	liú	to flow (4-3)
特 (牛)	tè	special (4-2)
爱 (爫)	ài	to love; love (4-4)
脑 (月)	nǎo	brain (4-1)
旅 (方)	lǚ	to travel (3-7)
热 (灬)	rè	hot (2-9)
烤 (火)	kǎo	to grill, to toast, to bake (4-2)
烧 (火)	shāo	to burn (3-8)
钱 (钅)	qián	money (2-6)
疼 (疒)	téng	to ache (3-8)
病 (疒)	bìng	sick, illness (3-8)
站 (立)	zhàn	station; to stand (3-3)
笑 (⺮)	xiào	to smile, to laugh, smile (4-4)
起 (走)	qǐ	to rise, to get up (3-9)

11 Strokes

Chinese (Radical)	Pinyin	English
假 (亻)	jià	holiday; leave of absence (3-7)
做 (亻)	zuò	to do, to make (2-2)
象 (⺈)	xiàng	appearance; elephant (4-2)
菜 (艹)	cài	dish, vegetable (1-11)
常 (⺌)	cháng	often (2-8)
得 (彳)	de	[degree, result of] (2-8)
	dé	to receive, to get (3-1)
	děi	have to, must (3-1)
馆 (饣)	guǎn	building (2-8)
寄 (宀)	jì	to send, to post, to mail (3-9)
骑 (马)	qí	to ride (bicycle or horse) (3-3)
绿 (纟)	lǜ	green (2-4)
球 (王)	qiú	ball (1-9)
望 (王)	wàng	to expect (4-2)
教 (夂)	jiāo; jiào	to teach (4-1)
晚 (日)	wǎn	evening, late (2-2)
您 (心)	nín	you [polite form] (2-7)
情 (忄)	qíng	feelings (4-4)
惯 (忄)	guàn	to get used to (4-2)
累 (田)	lèi	tired (4-3)
蛋 (疋)	dàn	egg (3-9)

Chinese	Pinyin	English
聊 (耳)	liáo	chat (4-1)
票 (西)	piào	ticket (3-4)
第 (竹)	dì	(order) (3-1)
着 (羊)	zhe	[grammatical word] (4-1)
雪 (雨)	xuě	snow (2-9)
黄 (黄)	huáng	yellow;
	Huáng	a surname (2-4)

12 Strokes

Chinese	Pinyin	English
舒 (人)	shū	comfortable (3-8)
就 (一)	jiù	merely; then, therefore (3-1)
谢 (讠)	xiè	to thank (2-8)
曾 (丷)	céng	once, formerly (4-3)
喜 (士)	xǐ	to like; happy (1-9)
喝 (口)	hē	to drink (1-11)
街 (彳)	jiē	street (4-4)
牌 (片)	pái	brand; plate, sign (4-3)
道 (辶)	dào	way (3-1)
晴 (日)	qíng	sunny, fine (2-9)
暑 (日)	shǔ	heat, hot weather (3-7)
最 (日)	zuì	the most (2-9)
渴 (氵)	kě	thirsty (1-11)
游 (氵)	yóu	to swim; to play (4-2)
期 (月)	qī	a period of time (2-1)
脾 (月)	pí	temper (4-3)
然 (灬)	rán	like that (4-1)
短 (矢)	duǎn	short (length) (3-6)
等 (竹)	děng	to wait (2-7)
黑 (黑)	hēi	black (2-4)

13 Strokes

Chinese	Pinyin	English
像 (亻)	xiàng	alike, to resemble (3-6)
蓝 (艹)	lán	blue (2-4)
数 (攵)	shù	numbers (3-1)
照 (灬)	zhào	to take (photos); photo (3-7)
新 (斤)	xīn	new (4-1)

Chinese	Pinyin	English
感 (心)	gǎn	to feel, sense (3-8)
想 (心)	xiǎng	to think (1-11)
错 (钅)	cuò	wrong, incorrect (2-1)
矮 (矢)	ǎi	short (height), low (height) (3-6)
意 (立)	yì	meaning (3-4)
路 (足)	lù	road (3-3)
跟 (足)	gēn	and (3-6)
零 (雨)	líng	small amount; zero (4-3)

14 Strokes

Chinese	Pinyin	English
境 (土)	jìng	area, situation (4-3)
赛 (宀)	sài	match, contest (3-4)
瘦 (疒)	shòu	thin, lean; tight (fitting) (3-6)
端 (立)	duān	up right (3-9)
算 (竹)	suàn	to calculate (3-7)
粽 (米)	zòng	dumpling (in bamboo leaves) (3-9)

15 Strokes

Chinese	Pinyin	English
影 (彡)	yǐng	movie, shadow (3-4)
题 (页)	tí	topic; question (4-4)

16 Strokes

Chinese	Pinyin	English
餐 (食)	cān	meal (4-3)
赞 (贝)	zàn	to support (4-4)
糕 (米)	gāo	cake, pudding (3-9)